'It's A

The 'dark art' o

E

Michael Layton & Stephen Burrows

Copyright 2018 by Michael Layton & Stephen Burrows. All rights reserved. This book or any portion thereof may not be reproduced or used in any manner whatsoever without the express written permission of the author(s) except for the use of brief quotations in a book review.

First published by Bostin Books in 2018

Find us on our Website **www.bostinbooks.co.uk** and our Facebook page *'Bostin Books'*

Dedication

To all of the police officers and staff in the UK who put themselves routinely in harm's way to protect us. The *'thin blue line'* - stretched but never broken.

Contents

Introduction

The *'art of blagging'* could be viewed by those outside Policing as conduct which was, and is, entirely inappropriate given the nature of the role. It cannot be denied that there is a thread of the darker side of human nature that runs through some of the stories in this book.

To some it is fun, an opportunity to 'let off steam' or simply 'one-upmanship' which at times borders on being downright cruel. The fact that it exists does prove though that police officers are only human after all.

To understand this sub-culture within the police service however, one has to look further than the act of 'pranking' itself, by asking the question, 'why does it exist at all'?

'Blagging', is not confined to one police force, rank, department, gender or geographical area. It permeates the whole police service, and indeed is present in other stressful roles: The Armed Forces, other Emergency Services, even the factory, where tricks such as telling the young apprentice to go to the shops and get some 'sky hooks' or a 'spirit level bubble' are prevalent.

A Psychologist could probably give a more scientific explanation, but it seems to us that *'blags'* act as a distraction from the more serious business of *'the job'* which was, and is, a hugely challenging and stressful profession. Police officers witness the very darkest aspects of humanity and it is therefore perhaps not surprising that *'dark humour'* follows, a communal *'letting off of steam',* a shared culture of finding humour in the hardest of circumstances.

There is also a belief that being a victim of *'blags'* is *'character forming'*. New and inexperienced colleagues are put through a series of 'tests', often with the honest intention of preparing them to safely face the ordeals to come: the sight of death and serious injury, abuse of many kinds, acts of perversion and evil, and the ever-present risk to themselves when confronting these issues.

Finally, one of the most important values sought in a fellow officer is trust that they will react positively in a crisis, won't freeze, or fail to support a colleague in trouble. *'Blagging'* is thought to 'harden up' and enable assessment of the likely reactions of a new team member when the 'chips are down'. It builds and bonds teams and encourages trust in each other.

Whether it be a probationer, a female officer, a CID officer, or a senior officer, there are few that would be able to say, during their service, that they were never truly *'taken in'* by a *'blag'*. It is an enduring feature of all policing, going back as far as memory permits. This little book is an attempt to preserve a few of the funniest tricks.

We have also included a number of stories, which do not involve *'blags'* but have been passed down over the years from generation to generation of police officer – no doubt some have been embellished along the way as they became enshrined in police folklore. Some appear in the collective memory of more than one force, and are now 'apocryphal' although no doubt stemming from one genuine source. A lot of police humour and stories is shared orally, in the tradition of the Greek poets, and grows in the telling, the exact truth buried in time.

For better or worse this book will hopefully provoke some smiles and laughs, whilst occasionally making some cringe and shake their heads with the extent and complexity of the tricks that officers, for the most part, played, and still play, on each other – albeit the growth of the politically correct 'police', a good thing in many ways, has had the effect of suppressing the *'art of the blag'*.

Above all, we hope to show the human face of policing – *'blagging'* does not replace the absolute requirement to protect the public at all times but it does add a layer of humour when the going gets tough.

The Stories

'The wrong beat'

In May of 1971, some British Transport Police officers attended the Home Office Training Centre at Bruche, Warrington, for a thirteen weeks Initial Training Course.

About half-way through the course one of them broke his leg, and for obvious reasons he was excused a number of duties including the morning parade. Parade in those days was a proper military-style affair: an inspection complete with marching to music boomed through speakers and across the Parade Square. The marching was often desperate, incurring the wrath of the 'drill pigs' who were usually chosen because they were ex-military and could actually march. The most frowned upon practice was 'tick-tacking' where inept individuals (one of the authors included), would, with flair and aplomb, manage the difficult feat of swinging an arm at the same time as the leg on the same side, instead of opposites. Cue much yelling and colourful language from the drill instructor.

To add further farce to the situation, the music, chosen for its marching beat, could occasionally provoke strange effects amongst the marchers, including a favourite at Ryton -On-Dunsmore Training Centre, John Philip Sousa's 'Liberty Bell', better known in Britain as the 'Monty Python' theme. 'Silly walks' could easily spread to 'silly marching'.

Back to the injured officer at Bruche, who was found gainful employment playing the marching record when given the signal by the 'drill pig'.

Unknown to the happy marchers, a couple of female officers from another intake had tampered with the scheduled playlist. When the signal was given to play the military march, the machine played the first few notes, then swiftly changed to the Beatles 'She loves you yeah, yeah'. The 'drill pig's' face was a red as a beetroot, he was absolutely fuming and came out with a string of expletives."

'Never forget your training'

"Whilst at the District Training Centre at Ryton on Dunsmore, a Staffordshire trainer told an officer that he was on foot patrol in the town centre when his attention was directed by alarmed members of the public to a very obese, (not the word used in those days), lady who had collapsed in the street with no signs of life.

This sort of incident can be as stressful to the officer attending as to the victim, with onlookers expecting professional First Aid to be rendered, whilst the officer is groping to remember what he was taught months or years previously, and which tended to involve a rubber doll called 'Resuscitation Annie'. This is one of those rare occasions where a rubber doll is preferable to practicing upon a human being!

Calling upon his first-aid training, and trying to look professional to the assembled crowd, the officer decided to kneel down close to the lady, and remembering the first rule of first-aid, *'speak to the patient to see if there is any sign of response'*, he said, *'are you alright my dear. Can you hear me?'*

There was no sign of life so he shuffled his knees a little closer to her and shook her a little, still hoping and praying for a response, but got nothing.

He shuffled his knees up really close to her so that they were now touching her body flanks. He leaned forward intending to put his cheek by her open mouth to see if he could feel the sensation of breath being exhaled, but as he did so the lady started to make some sounds, *"Ahhhh.....Ahhhh....Arhhhh."*

The officer, experiencing a rush of relief and gratitude for answered prayers said, *'Are you in pain my love?'* To which the obese woman replied, *'Yes, you're kneeling on my fat.'"*

'A few lessons in diversity'

"By the late 1990s the world of *'political correctness'* was advancing fast into the ranks of the training department at Tally Ho! Police Training Centre, Birmingham, with everyone walking on eggshells for fear of upsetting or offending others, although some could not quite get their heads around the concept...

On one occasion a particular trainer who was responsible for creating a course spotted a rather attractive lady giving a talk in a classroom, as an outside speaker.

After the session was concluded and the said blonde lady had gone, the trainer could not contain himself any further and bellowed to some of the other trainers in a corridor, *'who was that blonde chick in the class – she was a looker.'*

Some of the trainers were aghast and remonstrated with him saying, *'You can't say things like that.'*

Quick as a flash though, one of the other trainers seized the moment and with a serious face on said, *'that was my wife.'* Conversation finished.

Not quite learning his lesson, on another occasion the said trainer went to get his coat from a wardrobe in one of the offices at the end of a day's work. Another officer was sat in the office at the time and the trainer started to put part of his body inside the wardrobe and then proceed to jump in and out.

The officer looked blankly at him and asked what he was doing, to which he replied, *'I'm coming out of the closet!'* The officer continued to look blankly at him unamused.

His final faux pas came when he began researching domestic violence and realised that it was all related to assaults by males on females and that he needed to widen his knowledge to include attacks within the gay community.

He knew that there was a gay officer on the team and asked for some advice from a colleague as to whether it would be appropriate to discuss the issues with them. The response he got was, *'why don't you ask me? I lived with that officer for three years.'*

Third time unlucky! The length of his subsequent training career remains happily shrouded in the past."

'Rambo'

"Training schools were once run on strict military lines, with marching between classes, the saluting of senior officers, standing when speaking in class, and curfews at night.

One of the main aims of the curfew was to prevent illicit 'liaisons' between male and female officers. (In those days gay sex did not officially exist of course, especially amongst officers, so those fortunate enough to be gay and find a like-minded partner were ironically 'quids in' at training school.)

The sexes were segregated in separate accommodation blocks and the Instructors were known to prowl around at night, enforcing the curfew and dishing out punishment duties to miscreants.

One training intake featured a more mature recruit, clearly ex-military, who regaled classmates with tales of 'derring do' in the Falklands War. His favourite saying was *'I'm a rubber ball and you can't break me'*, whenever the militaristic 'squaddie' approach was applied by the Training Sergeants to the fresh-faced recruits. He claimed to have been in the Special Boat Service, but the general consensus was that he was 'bullshitting' about that to impress the ladies. For he was something of a philanderer and saw the female accommodation and its occupants as a pot of honey to be savoured.

And indeed, he soon struck up a relationship that he was keen to consummate. But how to get around the curfew? Easy. Dressed in dark clothing he approached the female block in stealth mode after curfew time and was seen to climb up the outside, using the mortar courses for handhold and then into an open upstairs window and the arms of his lover. Perhaps he was SBS then?"

'A word on the Probationary Period'

Prior to the very recent introduction of Direct Entry to the police at higher ranks, every officer, from Constable to Chief Constable, began as a 'Probationary Constable' better known as a *'Pro-Con'*. Probation lasted for two years, during which period dismissal was allowed if the recruit didn't come up to scratch. It is fair to say that every officer bears some scars, usually mental, from Probation, mainly caused by the relentless efforts of their colleagues to use, abuse and test them, for the reasons set out in the Introduction. Thus, Probation is a fertile ground for 'blags', as you will see.....

'Emergency Landing'

"A young PC on his first set of nights was told to relieve the controller at 2am so that the latter could have his break. He was told not to touch anything but just to listen to the radio and answer the phone. If there was any action required, all he needed to do was to ask the front-office man who was next door and very experienced.

He was then left on his own, and a few minutes later the phone rang. The probationer picked the phone up and the caller introduced himself as being an 'air traffic controller' from Birmingham Airport, who reported that a light plane was in trouble. The caller said that the plane was going to make an emergency landing on the local reservoir and that the officer needed to tell the senior officer on duty so that it could be cordoned off. The fire brigade and the ambulance service were on the way.

At this point the phone went dead.

The officer called out to the office-man but got no answer. He called out again and still there was no reply – he started to panic.

He eventually ran into the front-office, shouting for him, only to be met by a number of his so-called mates who fell about laughing at his panicked expression.

The *'air traffic controller'* turned out to be the office-man putting on an accent.'

A second incident of Air Traffic Control occurred at Acocks Green police station. The area covered by that station at that time included the Coventry Road in the Hay Mills area where there was a large stretch of open ground. In fact, that police area border nearly reached Birmingham airport, and aircraft coming in to land on flight paths above the Coventry Road were regular sights when on patrol.

In the early hours of one morning, when all was quiet, a young probationer was contacted on the radio and told to report urgently to the Inspector's office, which he duly did. He was issued with some special equipment and instructions, and hurried to a police vehicle which transported him speedily out to the open ground in Hay Mills.

He spent a happy hour with his issue table tennis bats watching the planes and awaiting his important role in assisting a plane in trouble to land on the open ground before realisation dawned."

'Now you see it – now you don't'

"A night shift 'test' in a more rural force, was to get one of the probationers to cycle out of town a couple of miles to a pre-determined point.

There they would wait for a *'Home Defence'* testing of flares that would be fired from the roof of the Police Station.

The victim of this particular test would then wait until they received a radio call, stating that the flare had been fired, and to report the sighting and colour of the flare. They were also led to believe that several other members of the shift were positioned as observers, at various locations around the town, to also report on the sighting and colour of the flare.

In reality, the rest of the shift was sitting having a cup of tea in the Control Room awaiting the fun, and the result of the test.

As you have probably guessed, it must be mentioned at this stage that there were no flares going to be fired from the roof, in fact the flares didn't exist. This was all about honesty under pressure.

At the allotted time, the Control Room stated a flare had been fired, and proceeded to call up the *'bogus observers'* who all duly reported back, *'yes a red flare seen,'* all except the victim probationer, who, when it got to his turn, and with disappointment in his voice, stated, *'I didn't see it.'*

He was questioned as to his exact location, direction he was looking, and whether he had been sleeping or otherwise shirking on duty.

Another flare was *'fired',* and again all the *'bogus'* observers reported, *'yes bright green, very visible,'* until again the *'victim'* reported, *'I didn't see it.'*

The Controller then gave the victim an ear-bending lecture about keeping awake, wasting everybody's time, and also the cost of the flares.

Another flare was *'fired',* again with positive sightings from the *'observers'* and this time, when it got around to the now worried young officer, he earnestly reported, *'Yes, red flare seen very clearly this time.'*

Drinks were on him at the next shift *'choir practice.'"* (For those who haven't read 'One In For D&D', our book of Police slang, 'choir practice' is early morning drinks after night shift).

'The bucket treatment'

One officer has memories of his time, with other recruits, as *'Pro-Cons'* at West Bromwich Police Station.

"We all got set up in turn. Sunday morning on earlies, (6am x 2pm shift), our tutor constable, or *'parent'* as they were known then, took us to the back door of the cell block in a panda car. West Bromwich *'nick'* was a five-storey building and the back door was directly overlooked by the landing windows.

We were told to press the bell and wait....three floors above us the bucket of water was made ready: on pressing the bell we were duly doused with cold water with shouts of *"Welcome to West Brom, 'sprog.'*

One lad actually had his pocket note book out as he waited, the water rearranged that nicely I recall."

'Swimming in the Cut'

A Black Country tale. An officer based at Bloxwich Sub-Division recollects:

"We were always *'up for a laugh'* and we often pulled stunts – or *'blags'* as we called them. New recruits were called probationers, because they were subject of a two-year probationary period during which time, if deemed unfit by senior officers, they could be dismissed. They often found themselves on the receiving end of these *'blags'*.

There was another more serious side to it though, as it also gave the regular officers, the ones who were going to work with the probationers, a 'feel' for them, to see what they were made of.

How they reacted to the *'blags'* gave us a yardstick as to how they'd react under pressure.

I recall one such incident with a probationer who was a 6-foot-tall strapping lad, about twenty years of age at the time, very fit, and if I recall correctly, played for a football team. He seemed to fit in straight away and some of us agreed he'd be good for a laugh, so we agreed to set up a *'blag'* for him.

He had seen others being set up by other officers, understood it went on, and was quite proud of the fact that he'd managed to avoid being 'caught' despite several attempts, so I devised a plan.

It took quite some time to set up as it had to involve every member of our shift, and the controller. It took about a week to get the details and the equipment we needed in place plus, what we intended to do could only be done when we were on night duty as we needed to put it into action when it was fairly quiet, and dark, so we had to wait for night shifts to roll around.

I tasked a couple of officers to gather equipment and to manufacture a 'dummy' that would be mistaken for a person from a distance, would float, and had to be wearing certain clothing, right down to its shoes.

I also had to brief a member of the public, who was a friend of mine, who lived on my 'patch' to help us. When I explained what it was about, he jumped at the chance.

So, nights came around and I'd arranged that the officer would be working with me on this particular night. This wasn't suspicious as 'pairs' were often swapped around for experience.

This was a Sunday night, the last night of our tour of duty, chosen as it was also usually the quietest night of the shift. What the officer didn't know was that a little later that night, we would take a report over the radio from our Controller about a missing person. The very precise details about that missing person's description, age, sex, height, clothing worn, (including shoes), habits and favourite haunts were duly noted by him when they were passed over the air.

Nothing more was said about this until hours later into our shift, when, at around 3am, a report came over the radio that a member of the public had called in, complaining about strange noises being heard on the canal towpath at the back of his house, which was quite near to a canal bridge.

Off we went to the complainant's house, who duly informed us of hearing strange noises like splashing and shouting at the rear of his house - it had woken him up and he wasn't happy.

We duly went to the canal bridge adjacent to the house and walked onto the canal towpath.

As we walked along the towpath, there in front of us, on the side near the water was a pair of shoes! Not just any old shoes, but shoes matching the description of the ones worn by the missing person reported earlier this night.

I mentioned this in passing to my colleague who readily agreed with me.

Then, silhouetted in our dim torch light, he spotted a body floating face down, near to the opposite bank. At this point he started to get very animated and informed the Controller that there was a body in the canal.

I took a bit of a back seat to see what he was going to do, but was pre-empted by the Controller asking him if there was any sign of life?

He replied that the body hadn't been checked.

The prompt reply came back, *'Well you bloody well better hurry up and do so, he might be still alive.'*

'What we going to do?' the probationer asked me.

'We?' I said. *'Me, nothing, however, you're gonna jump in and go and grab him.'*

'Me, why me?' He asks.

'Because I'm the senior officer here, and you're younger and fitter than me, now bloody hurry up, he might still be alive!'

Unknown to the officer, some other officers were in hiding, in the long grass opposite the *'body'*, poised with cameras.

He hurriedly 'stripped off' a bit, not too much, just enough, and lowered himself into the cold dark water and waded chest deep over to the *'body'*.

Just as he put his hand on it and turned it face up to see it was nothing more than a mop head with a wig on, with poly containers made up to wear a coat, the canal was lit up with camera flashes and *'hoots'* of laughter.

He was not amused and the air turned blue, with threats of revenge to those involved. To give him his due though he dragged the *'body'* back to shore.

Just to show we were compassionate, we let him go home early to shower and change.

Strangely enough, upon returning to work a few days later, nothing was said about it - but he never bragged about not being caught ever again.

A few fake swimming certificates and a fake life-saving award from the Humane Society were handed out to him on parade much to everyone's amusement - and with a round of applause."

'A part on 'The Bill''

A probationer from 'F Division', Steelhouse Lane, in Birmingham City Centre, remembered this excellent *'blag'* up to the day she retired, having completed thirty-years police service, and even told the story in her retirement speech:

"Whilst a probationer on the 999 response at The Lane, the shift Inspector called me into the office one day along with another female officer.

The conversation went something like this:

'Right girls, I have picked my two favourite girls, do you fancy being on television? It's an episode of 'The Bill'.

What we want is for you to attend a location next Sunday where a film crew will be present. All they want you to do is walk like they do on the opening scene of 'The Bill'.

You will have to practice the walk but you just need to 'plod along' like they do on 'The Bill'. The feet just slowly walking along the cobbled streets.'

Seemed easy we thought!

He said that the film-crew would be set up on Livery Street the following Sunday morning. The *'gaffer'* wanted us to be immaculate as we were being filmed, so we had to *'bull'* (polish) our shoes to be like mirrors, and our skirts had to be pressed to perfection.

He queried, *'Were we up for the job? Were we ready to represent the 'F' Division on national television?'*

We responded, *'Too right we are gaffer – you've picked the right girls for the job!'*

The Inspector said that he wanted us in his office for 1.30pm, ready for the 2-10pm shift on the day, with tunics pressed and looking immaculate.

Because we were extremely excited, we told the whole shift that we had been picked to appear on an episode of *'The Bill'* and a starring character would be the comedian Les Dennis.

The shift looked really pleased for us.

So as the days passed, I went home every day and pressed my skirt with paper. This was a good old-fashioned way back then of ensuring maximum crease in the skirt. I *'bulled'* my shoes with polish, spitting on them endlessly and sat watching late night television *'bulling'* my shoes until I could see my face in them.

During the course of that week both myself, and the other officer, went on parade for our shifts and the *'gaffer'* announced to everybody that we were going to be on the television. He even got members of the CID to attend our parade to enjoy the moment and he invited the two of us to practice *'our walk '* as they did on *'The Bill'*.

We enjoyed walking in front of the shift and members of the CID in the parade room at Steelhouse Lane, showing the shift how we had practiced our walk and how good we were going to be on national TV. They could certainly be very proud of us! The Inspector said that he had a better idea – there was a short ramp in the station yard -down to the rear bar area, which was cobbled, and for maximum effect he invited us in front of the shift to walk down the cobbled stones pretending we were walking on *'The Bill'* so that the whole shift and CID could see.

I look back now and cringe!

So, the big day came – it was a Sunday and I arrived for work with my tunic, skirt and everything else I wore pressed - my shoes were gleaming.

The other officer looked pretty smart too.

The Inspector arranged for the *'Zulu'* vehicle to pick us up and take us to the camera shoot area on Livery Street where he dropped us off. The Inspector told us to look out for Les Dennis and that he would tell us what to do and where to go. 'How exciting', I thought to myself – this was it! I was finally going to be famous. I was eventually going to be 'spotted'. Perhaps a career in film and TV was waiting.

I saw the Force helicopter hovering above, and was told over the radio that this had been arranged by the Inspector just for us!

So, we walked around this area which was rough ground with lots of camera crews about. There were swanky mobile units full of camera equipment, and a catering facility and this was most definitely a film-set. I was getting really excited.

Then I saw Les Dennis!

'Oh my God', I thought to myself, this is it. Without further ado, I walked right up to him and with a huge big smile on my face said, *'Hi Les, I think you are expecting us.'*

He looked at me as if I was *'nuts'* and said, *'I haven't got a clue what you are on about.'* I continued to rattle on, oblivious.

'We are here for the walk-on part for 'The Bill'.'

I thought for one moment that perhaps his Personal Assistant would know more, but Les Dennis said,

'Look, if you want me to sign your note-book that is no problem but I know nothing about 'The Bill'. We aren't here for that, we are doing a documentary about canals and you are here to simply guard the expensive equipment lying around because this is a right dodgy area.'

Well *'the penny'* started to slowly drop and then I heard something over my personal radio. I can't remember the comment but I thought to myself this is a bloody *'blag'*!

I had worked all week pressing my uniform, cleaning my shoes, walking in front of the shift, walking in front of the CID, pretending to walk like *'The Bill',* only to find out that we were the security for the camera equipment.

The other officer was fuming as the shift started commenting. and I could tell that the radio operator was in absolute stitches and could hardly talk.

We walked all the way back to the police station only to be greeted by the shift who clapped and cheered when we walked into Steelhouse Lane.

That work shift went by very slowly, and I was still 'gob-smacked'. The Inspector then invited us to go for a beer at the pub at the top of Steelhouse Lane.

I remember being in the changing rooms at the police station and the other officer refused to go. I told her she had to – it was seen as *'fun'* nothing more and nothing less, and if they knew that it had upset her, she would be fair game for future *'blags'*.

She still refused to go for a drink but I got the Inspector to buy my beer all night, along with other members of the shift.

'Community Service'

"In the days when Divisional Orders, (written information and Orders notices from HQ), were sent out to Section Stations, we had a *'know-it-all sprog'* arrive at Holyhead Road.

Some of the lads created a *'spoof'* Order to the effect that the Chief Constable had authorised each Division to nominate a junior police constable to attend a youth seminar at Birmingham Council House, where people from industry and local government departments would engage with one another.

The fake Order stated that our new *'sprog'* had been selected and that he should attend the Council House in best uniform at an appointed time and date to take part.

Off he duly went only to find that the security officer at the Council House hadn't got a clue what he was on about"

'Where's the fire?'

"When I worked in Birmingham City Centre there was a regular *'blag'* that was played on new probationers.

There used to be a Gas Showroom in the High Street and on nights when it was quiet a radio message would go out to the officer, *'There's a report of a fire at the Gas Showroom please attend.'*

The young officer would duly attend and report that there were no fires there only to get the response, *'What about the ones in the window?'*

The other trick that officers who were driving cars used to play on them was to stop and ask them if they wanted to jump in for a break, and each time they went to open the door of the car it would be moved forward a few inches until eventually they gave up."

'The proof house shooting'

"In hindsight I'm amazed at some of the things we got up to. We never thought twice, everyone was *'blagging'* everyone else and we had all fallen for one or more at some stage in our careers. You would probably get the sack for some of them nowadays.

One regular theme was the *'bottle test'*. There were a variety of ingenious tricks contrived all over the place to see how a young officer would react when faced with a potentially life-threatening incident. The belief was that having the experience in a 'safe' environment would better prepare a probationer for when, God forbid, the real thing occurred.

Steelhouse Lane's policing area covered what was known as the 'Gun Quarter' in Birmingham, which contained the 'Proof House, a building of great antiquity.

The Proof House was established in 1813 by an Act of Parliament at the request and expense of the then prosperous Birmingham Gun Trade. It provided a testing and certification service for firearms in order to prove their quality of construction under firing conditions.

Such testing prior to the sale or transfer of firearms was made mandatory by the Gun Barrel Proof Act of 1868, which made it an offence to sell, offer for sale, transfer, export or pawn an un-proofed firearm, with certain exceptions for military organisations. Thus, this building contained firearms and ammunition, and its security was a very big deal. All alarm calls were treated very seriously indeed.

Steelhouse Lane had a number of what you would call 'riot vans', which were used for late-night City Centre patrols, scooping up drunks and 'scufflers'. It was discovered by a shift member that one particular van could be made to misfire loudly upon demand. It sounded just like a gunshot......hang on a minute.

In the wee small hours on the next set of nights a 'double crewed' patrol car comprising an experienced officer and a 'Pro-Con' was directed to a 'shout' at The Proof House – a report of persons breaking in. They arrived first, and the experienced officer told the younger officer to wait at the front, whilst he disappeared along the alley at the side, providing a running commentary that could be heard by all. *'There's someone here, I'm in pursuit, he's got a gun',* – *'BANG',* then total silence.

The Controller started demanding information from the Probationer, who must have been both stunned and frightened, with everybody listening to the response. The 'test' was passed, but in hindsight was a step too far. The Probationer probably never really forgave the 'mature' officer, the van driver who had provoked the misfire from the van parked at the rear of The Proof House with precise and immaculate timing, or indeed the rest of the shift."

'It's in the DNA'

"Back in 2003, a new *'sprog'* started on the shift, and although he was a really good lad he was very *'cocky'* and needed bringing down *'a peg or two'*.

For a few months he had been warned about his conduct around the *'old sweats'*, playing tricks, only for him to reply, *'Ah it's okay. I've plenty more up my sleeve'*

One day, whilst crewed up with him, we were sent to a crime-scene watch. (Guarding a crime scene for Forensics). After about an hour he decided that he was desperate for the toilet and started dancing about in pain.

Knowing that there was absolutely nowhere for him to go I suggested he went to the rear of the premises out of public view, which he duly did.

Whilst waiting I had a *'light-bulb moment'* and hatched a plan.

A few days later I contacted Scenes of Crime officers and enquired whether they had a form to complete if *'DNA'* was recovered from a crime-scene.

They confirmed that they did and I duly explained that the *'sprog'* had needed to have a *'pee'* at the scene and could they send a *'blag'* form to him outlining that his *'DNA'* had been found and asking him to explain how it had got there.

Some months later I had forgotten about the plan, but whilst on parade I noticed the *'sprog'* opening some post. There was a look of confusion on his face and he kept putting it away and then opening the letter again to read it before looking around the room.

After the parade finished, he asked to speak to the Sergeant, following which I was asked to look after him whilst he made a statement.

The Sergeant spoke to me on my own and explained why and the penny dropped.

I explained to the Sergeant that it was a *'blag'* and he went along with it. I took the probationer off and stressed that he needed to do a very detailed statement including which hands were used etc. and the fact that the Detective Inspector would need to review it and consult with the Crown Prosecuting Solicitors.

He duly completed a two-page statement with full details and handed it to the Sergeant who waited until 4am on nights before handing him the statement in a frame and the words, *'Never blag a blagger.'"*

'Eye see it'

"In the mid-eighties at Bournville Lane a lad joined my shift.

His brother was in the job and every time you tried to tell him something he'd say,

'Yes, I know, my brother has told me.'

Then you would go to show him something else and he would say, *'Yes I know, my brother has told me all about that'.* This became rather irritating. He was far too big for his boots.

It was a cold January and we were on a week of nights. One of the lads went to an abattoir during the day and obtained a bucket of entrails.

At about 2am, having briefed the Force Control Room that it was a *'blag'*, two probationers, including the one who knew everything, were radioed at the end of their refreshment break to go to Cob Lane, Bournville near to the entrance to the police station overflow car park. There was a report of someone being attacked.

They ran to the scene and the probationer who knew everything saw something in his torchlight. The radio call goes in, *'Bravo Two control. We have a large quantity of human tissue here and lots of body parts. I think we are dealing with a murder.'*

The Inspector and Night DC attended, and the probationer taped it all off and started a scene log.

At about 4.30am the hapless probationer radioed up, *'Bravo Two. I've found an eye. It's definitely human.'*

At 6am we all drove down Cob Lane past him on our way home.

In the last car was one of the Sergeants who stopped and handed him a bucket, *'It's a 'blag'. Clean that 'shit' up and go home.'*

For months afterwards *'bobbies'* who he didn't know would walk up to him and say *'I've found an eye!'"*

There is something about graveyards and cops.....'

'A battered bedsheet'

"Weoley Castle Cemetery – there was always a trick to get the new recruit to walk through on nights to a false report of someone screaming. As the recruit walked through someone dressed in a suit or a mask would jump out.

On this particular night recruit *'A'* was sent in from one side, whilst his partner came in from the other side. Five minutes beforehand, a colleague hid himself in the middle of the crematorium wearing a white bed-sheet.

As the *'new boy'* approached, out jumped the white-sheeted figure, screaming like a demented banshee, whereupon the new boy drew his *'peg'* and *'hammered several bells of shit'* out of his *'ghost'* colleague'.

Lesson learnt – never jump out on an ex-paratrooper!"

'Graveyard Tale 2'

"A young PC was doing a set of nights, with his tutor constable, when they were told to investigate suspicious behavior in a very *'spooky'* and dark churchyard.

On arrival, the tutor officer told the probationer to go one way, whilst he went the other, and then promptly ran off leaving the young officer on his own.

The young officer nervously made his way through the churchyard and then in the distance he saw two ghostly figures flitting between the gravestones making *'whooing'* noises. The officer turned around and ran back to the *'panda'* car and locked himself in.

He refused to get out of the car even when the tutor returned and explained that the ghostly figures were in fact two members of the shift dressed in white traffic coats."

'Graveyard Tale 3'

"Graveyards and *'blags'* go together like fish and chips, and the 'F Division' had two of the very best - in Hockley, at Warstone Lane and Key Hill.

Warstone Lane Cemetery contains actual catacombs, and is very creepy, whilst Key Hill is the oldest cemetery in Birmingham and is the final resting place of many notable figures in the city's history.

None of which meant anything to the shift members clustered on top of the multi-story car park overlooking the cemeteries. It was the graveyard shift, 3am, when biorhythms dip below zero, very little is happening, and something is required to enliven things.

The single-crewed probationer arrived below, following a report of suspicious activity in the graveyard, and the onlookers witnessed him embarking on a thorough, if tentative, search by torchlight. Suddenly a shrouded figure leapt out from behind a grave.

A foot-chase commenced, accompanied by much shrieking. Except it was the 'ghost' in pursuit, right across the cemetery, much to the amusement of the crowd above. Once again, a bedsheet and Halloween mask had done the trick!"

'Graveyard Tale 4'

"A *'blag'* that had our unit in stiches. It was the early hours of the morning, and the *'Pro Con'* was out on single foot patrol in Birmingham City Centre.

We got two older PC's to dress in black, whiten their faces with makeup, and hide behind tombstones in St Martins churchyard.

Having focused in the CCTV cameras to record the event, the *'Pro-Con'* was directed to investigate a report of suspicious activity in the graveyard.

He was filmed gingerly approaching, and slowly walking between the tombs. Suddenly, our two old salts leapt up in front of him screaming maniacally.

The *'Pro-Con'* extended his arm, holding his illuminated torch out in front of him and waving it about like a light sabre whilst backing away at speed. Our two old salts collapsed in laughter.

The *'Pro-Con'* was last seen disappearing fast. The film was a big hit when shown to all and sundry later.

'Graveyard Tale 5'

"At Chelmsley Wood, circa 1998, there was a female officer who would often openly say, *'I don't mind admitting it, I get 'shit scared' on nights. I know we're supposed to be brave going around the back of premises looking for burglars but I'm always 'shitting myself.'*

Another officer on the shift bought a rubber face mask that looked like a gnarly old man, a very authentic human face mask. He also bought a big black cloak.

He then looked at the postings and saw that the female officer was working with another male colleague the following night.

He got hold of him, and took him to Castle Bromwich graveyard where he showed him a footpath leading through the graveyard which passed a five-feet tall, very old, gravestone. The other officer was then briefed as follows, *'At about 3am tomorrow you will get a job at this location. Bring her this way, and when you get here, make sure that she is in front of you.'*

At 3am a job came in over the radio, *'Lima Mike...can you go to Castle Bromwich churchyard, a local says that a figure dressed in dark clothing is acting furtively in the graveyard. Can you check it out please?'*

They got there and the female officer was not happy at all and made no secret of it.

Her male colleague also said that he was scared, and said, *'In fact I'm going to get my CS spray ready.'* He duly took out his CS, (tear gas canister), shook it up, and held it in his hand.

His female colleague followed suit and they moved on along the path, although as instructed, he dropped back slightly.

They reached the large gravestone and a dark figure leaped out screaming.

The female officer began screaming and emptied a whole can of CS spray onto the phantom figure!

Later at the *'nick'*, she said to her colleagues, *'I'm there screaming, this thing is on the floor and I look around and my partner is doubled up, laughing his head off.'*

The perpetrator of the *'blag'* was helped back to the police station and left to sit in the back-yard for two hours, recovering from the effects of the gas, before being taken home. There is a moral in there somewhere.'

'You can count on me'

"It was a cold and miserable night, especially for a young probationary constable, who we shall call 'Officer A', who was on lone foot patrol in Birmingham City Centre.

I pulled up alongside her in *'Foxtrot Zulu 1'* and the conversation went as follows:

Me 'Hello' A', you look frozen, fancy a warm in the car?'

'A' 'You are a life saver. But what if the gaffer catches me?'

Me 'He won't, on a miserable night like this, he will be in his office.'

I then proceeded to drive around the City with the heater turned up and after about fifteen minutes I suddenly said, *'Shit! It's the Gaffer coming towards us.'*

She replied, *'Keep going, and don't let him catch me.'*

Me 'I can't do that. Lie on the floor in the back and put my coat over you, keep as still as you can, and don't make a sound, it will be fine.'

I pulled up next to the Inspector and said, *'Hello Gaffer, I didn't expect to see you out on a horrible night like thi*s.'

He said, *'I fancied a drive around. I was looking for the 'A'. She is posted to the City, but I haven't come across her yet.'*

Me. *'I am not surprised; she's hiding on the floor in the back, with my coat pulled over her head. She just jumped in as I pulled up alongside her and then refused to get out.'*

She lifted her head up and responded, *'You bastard, ……… Hello Gaffer!'*

The Inspector was trying hard not to smile and tried to impose his authority by ordering her out of the vehicle.

I said, *'Bloody 'Sprogs', eh Gaffer, what are they like. I'll leave it with you.'*

The female officer said, *'You're still a bastard.'"*

'There are two sides to the story'

"I told the above story at my retirement do.

I was walking my beat freezing cold and I saw headlights approaching and was relieved to see it was the *'Zulu'*.

I leant in to speak to *X* and I could feel the heat from the car heater.

He said, *'Do you want to get warm?'*

The offer was too good to refuse so I climbed into the back. I was chattering away with my head between the driver's seat and the passenger's seat where *X's* partner was sitting.

Suddenly I saw the supervision car coming.

I shouted, *'Shit'* and *X* told me to lie down on the back seat and cover myself whilst he spoke to them.

The Inspector and Sergeant, (Steve Burrows), approached, and one of them said to him, *'Evening X. It's a cold night, anything happening, whose walking this beat tonight?'*

X turned his head to the back and said, *'is this your beat?'*

I shot upright, smiled and said *'Hi gaffer.'*

'X' stitched me the bastard.'"

'Sergeant Pepper's Lonely Hearts Club Band'

"A probationer at Erdington was tasked to walk in front of the annual Salvation Army parade as it made its way along Erdington High Street and back to its headquarters in Station Road.

He was given the route and a pair of white gloves to enhance his appearance then duly marched in front of the brass band about ten yards ahead as instructed.

As they got further along the High Street the officer noticed that the band played quieter and then was almost inaudible. The officer was marching for all his worth and giving a good display in front of the happy shoppers, who were standing on the pavements watching him marching up the middle of the road.

What the officer didn't realise was that the reason for the band playing so quietly was due to the fact that they had turned off left along a different route that he had been told to adhere to.

He was left marching alone up the carriageway for another two hundred yards in the face of oncoming traffic and some very perplexed members of the public".

'Another emergency landing'

"New recruits were often sent on the roof of the flats near to Bromford Lane at night with a torch to guide the planes into Birmingham Airport as the landing lights had failed.

They would be there for hours waving at the planes coming in to land."

'On the buses'

"I recall a story in the mid-1970's. It was the morning of April 1st and a more experienced officer was on duty, working nights, doubled up on *'Alpha Mike 9'* panda, together with a very young *'Pro Con'* who had just finished his twelve-week initial training course.

At about 4.30am the officers drove into John Bright Street and, as was the norm, three or four 'night service' buses were parked up at their terminus. As the officers drove past, the opportunity for an *'April Fool'* joke arose as the mischievous element of the older officer's character came to the surface.

The officers pulled up in front of the leading bus and looking very official, with caps on, and carrying a clipboard, they boarded the bus and spoke to the driver who was reading his newspaper.

The older officer established that he was addressing Driver 'X' from Liverpool Street Garage and after consulting his clipboard said,

"It's nothing to worry about driver, it's just that we have had a message from your garage to say that you have got to change your route from the 61, 62, or 63 to the number 13 route, which is usually out of Yardley Wood garage.
They are short on drivers and can't get the service running properly."

The bus driver protested that he didn't know what the number 13 route was, but a very helpful passenger at the back of the bus told him that he did and described where he had to go. And off they went.

Remember, it was *'April Fool's* day."

'Meeting the Chief'

"A very naïve probationer, who later became an Inspector, was posted to our shift – he asked far too many questions!

I was asked to keep an eye on him and *'train him up'.*

I was busy, with places to go and people to see, and the last thing I wanted was a *'sprog'* on my coat tails, so I arranged for him to do a few days in the Front Office, answering the phone, making entries in the Minor Occurrence Book, and dealing with the *'SFQ',s* (Silly Fucking Questions), at the counter, which was also known as *'batting practice'*! Anything to get him away from me!

On the desk in the Front Office, were the two normal grey enquiry telephones and a bright red telephone, which stood out.

One day the officer said, '*What's the red phone for?*'

I said, '*Well, every enquiry office throughout the force has a red phone. It is the Chief Constable's hot line. If that rings, you stop what you are doing, answer it immediately, and deal accordingly. I wouldn't worry too much about that, it hardly ever rings.*'

The *'red phone'* was actually a link with Bridge Street West Police station, which was not a 24-hour station and had an old police phone box outside. Out-of-hours, you could pick this phone up and it would divert you to the *'red phone'*. The local beat lads had put an *'out of order'* sticker on it ages before, to stop the drunks from using it, although it worked perfectly well.

After a couple of weeks, I arranged for the probationer to be in the Front Office again, it would be about 10.30 in the morning.

At 10.45am exactly, the office-man left the office to make a cup of tea, leaving the *'Pro-Con'* on his own in the office. At that point, I picked up the phone outside Bridge Street West, which activated the red telephone on the desk in the front office at Steelhouse Lane police station.

'Ring, Ring' – *'Hello, PC ......speaking, can I help you Sir?'*

Me, (aka: Chief Constable Geoffrey Dear), *'The very man, Chief Constable here. Is your pocket book up to date? If not make sure that it is. You have a staff appraisal with me at 11 o'clock, come to the 7th floor at Lloyd House and don't be late.'*

I hung up before he could say anything else.

Apparently, he was last seen running up Steelhouse Lane towards Lloyd House!"

'The mortuary *'blag'* and *'double-blag''*

"A *'double blag'* is a *'blag'* that builds on a *'blag'*, usually rebounding on the original *'blagger'*.

The *'Mortuary blag'* is practiced throughout the Police Service. It is very simple, but effective. The new officer is told that, as part of their training, they are to pay a visit to the Mortuary (in Newton Street, Birmingham in this case), and see a number of dead bodies in various states, close up and personal.

This is in fact a true statement, or was at one time. It was thought to be a good preparation for trainee officers to see death, (for the majority for the first time), in a 'safe' environment, before coming across it in a real situation in the many forms it presents itself to police officers.

This, a potentially traumatic and worrying prospect for the Probationer, was built up as highly as possible by his 'mates', and then the victim was escorted to the Mortuary. The pre-warned Mortuary Assistant would let them in and commence the tour. Bodies on shiny tables, covered in sheets, as seen on T.V. Bodies in drawers, and of course, one body under a sheet suddenly sat up and moaned....

The mortuary *'Double Blag'* goes like this. The victim of the original *'blag'* is told that this time they can play the body under the sheet. They are of course very keen, desirous of being in with the *'inner-circle'* on the shift, and to play the trick on the next victim.

So off they go to the Mortuary and set themselves up amongst the bodies, with the help of their fellow officers of course and are left alone to await the arrival of a new recruit

There they lie, alone, amongst the dead. It is very quiet, the quiet of the dead. Nobody comes.

Suddenly their arm is gripped from a neighbouring gurney, and a there is a voice where there should be none. *'It's fucking cold in here ain't it?'* This works best if the victim is lying in a drawer......head injuries have occurred."

'Mortuary *'Blag'* three'

"A new officer was told that to frighten a fellow probationer he could climb into a gurney cabinet and pretend to be a body for the officer to find. He thought it was a brilliant idea.

He climbed in and it was all arranged that the other officer would be in 'in a minute'. Then when the drawer was opened, he would jump out...All the lights were turned off and he was left.....for a long time.

After almost two hours the radio went off, *'I'm still being a body, but it's very cold now, can I come out?'*

The Inspector went to rescue him."

'Dealing with the dead'

"Although I later became a West Midlands Police officer, when I first joined I was a young bobby in the County and among the many things that you were expected to do was to deal with deceased individuals – you were in effect your own Coroner's Officer.

In those days you were single-crewed, and one night just before Christmas I was on mobile patrol when I was directed by the Controller to attend the local mortuary to deal with a body which was being taken there by ambulance.

The person concerned was an elderly gentleman who had collapsed and died at a carol service.

The Controller said that if I was lucky the ambulance crew would help me.

The mortuary was a very old Victorian building on the edge of town and it was the last place that I wanted to be. If I set the scene, it was late on, raining heavily, and very spooky.

As I approached the mortuary the ambulance was just leaving, and, having flashed their headlights, they disappeared off into the night.

I was relieved however, to find that there was a Police Cadet there, who had been doing an attachment to the Ambulance Service, and had been told to remain to assist me.

Apart from booking the body in, it was my responsibility to undress the corpse and to take possession of all items of property and bag them up.

I asked the Cadet if he had ever undressed a corpse before, and much to my surprise, he told me that he hadn't. Not wishing to show my inexperience I suggested that we sit the body up on the mortuary slab, and whilst one held it, the other removed the clothing.

'Sods law', the corpse was fully-dressed, including a heavy overcoat and a three-piece suit.

I took the initiative and said that I would sit him up and that the Cadet could remove the clothing.

The deceased was lying on his back on the mortuary slab and I bent over him from the top and put my hands under his arms. In doing so, as I leant over him, my tie came out of my tunic and went directly into his mouth, which was wide open – I knew that this was not going well.

I retrieved my tie, pushed it inside my shirt, and once again took up my position over the corpse. As I leant forward my face was only a matter of inches away from his face.

I started to raise him up when suddenly there was this load noise, almost like a roar, which came directly from the deceased. I nearly *'crapped'* myself, dropped the body, and ran out of the mortuary.

I ran out into the roadway, closely followed by the Cadet.

I made it clear that there was no way that I was going to go back in.

The Cadet was killing himself laughing, and I asked him what he thought was so funny. He explained that whilst the body was being transported in the ambulance that it had made a number of similar noises and that the ambulance crew had informed him that it was just 'air' escaping from the body.

After a couple of minutes, I finally summoned up the courage to go back inside and finish the job.

I took the valuables back to the *'nick'* and found that another PC was dealing with the deceased's family. They were in an interview room and I went in to find the officer asking how they would like the body to be dealt with.

They explained that they were themselves undertakers, at which point the very sensitive and caring officer said, *'I suppose it will be a DIY job then?'*

This wasn't to be my only brush with the mortuary.

When you were on earlies it was your job to go to the mortuary on a Tuesday morning and to take the bodies awaiting post-mortem out of the fridge, put the heating on and leave them to defrost before the pathologist arrived.

Again, whilst very young in service I went with a more experienced PC to carry out this task.

We arrived at the mortuary shortly after 6am and commenced moving the bodies out of the fridge. It was not uncommon to have four or more bodies.

On this occasion one of the corpses was a lady and after taking her out of the fridge we were required to put her on the *'slab'*. On this occasion I was at the feet end and my colleague was at the top.

As we picked the body up, the body lifted, but the deceased's hair remained on the tray. My colleague screamed and ran out. I was obliged to go and find him in order that we could finish the task.

I must say that in those days we were expected to carry out these duties as part of our work, without any protective clothing or gloves – just a really unpleasant task that we were expected to cope with."

'The Cycling Proficiency Test'

"Another one from Acocks Green. The *'Pro-Con'* was told that, now he or she had got a few months in, they were fit to be given a new and special responsibility. They would be the shift 'recoverer' of stolen bicycles. But before they could be of use performing this essential function, they had to pass a test for insurance purposes.

It was all set up during the early hours of the morning on the next set of night shifts. The back yard of the station was kitted out with tricky slaloms of cones and the shift assembled to cheer the candidate on. A Sergeant officiated, resplendent with clipboard, and set a series of tests, completed on a bicycle temporarily 'liberated' from lost property, the more mismatched the size of the rider to the bike, the better. It was possible to get several run-throughs of the course before realisation dawned. If it didn't, there was a certificate to be issued to the proud recipient on parade the next day."

'Shergar'

"When the famous racehorse *'Shergar'* went missing I did a fake telex message from the Garda, (Irish Police), saying that they had received good information that a consortium of Irish 'villains', based in Birmingham, were responsible.

The 'information' was to the effect that the horse was being kept in the Small Heath/ Sparkbrook/ Sparkhill area and that they were requesting discreet enquiries in the Irish community for information.

The Detective Inspector booked the telex to an officer who took it 'hook, line and sinker'. He was claiming *'spent with's'* and *'paid to's'*, (Expenses in connection with use of Informants), for several months re *'enquiries re Shergar'* and we were leaving him messages from numerous *'sarbut's'*, (Police slang for Informants), about possible leads.

Half the Irish publicans and staff in the locality were in on the *'blag'* and played their parts.

The officer eventually did an early morning raid on some land at the back of the Sydenham pub where he had been told they were keeping *'Shergar'*.

The only horses he found were some pit-ponies left there by some gypsies.

He only found out it was a *'blag'* when we had a visit from the Assistant Chief Constable Crime, along with members of the Police Committee, and he introduced the officer with, *'This is DS .... who has been looking for 'Shergar' but I think he should now be told it was a 'blag' because it is costing the job too much.'*

The officer was not a happy man!"

'This Chow Mein is wubbery'

"On the 'F' Division, (Birmingham City Centre), there was a certain *'larger than life'* Detective Sergeant who was renowned for his large appetite. He came into the office one night with a very large chicken chow mein, placed it on his desk and wandered off to the loo – a big mistake!

A certain DC proceeded to cut up a number of elastic bands and mixed them into the Chow Mein whilst everyone sat back and waited. The DS returned and tucked in heartily to his meal which he devoured with relish. At the conclusion he wiped his lips and said what a beautiful meal it was. No-one said a word."

'Brown nosing'

"When I was on the Operational Support Unit, about 1989/90, I was on *'Uniform Lima'*, (the Solihull van).

Because we used to work the football on a Saturday, we used to get a day off in the week, usually a Tuesday or a Wednesday.

I was supposed to be on weekly leave on this particular Wednesday, but had a last -minute court warning at Solihull Magistrates on the Wednesday morning. Rather than put my uniform on, I decided to go to court in a suit and tie.

I got to court only to be told that my defendant had changed his plea to guilty and I was no longer required...that used to happen quite often.

Oh well, five hours overtime for nothing, thank you very much!

One of my best mates who worked with me as a PC at Bradford Street Police Station, when I joined the force in 1981, was now a Detective Sergeant, in fact Acting Detective Inspector, at Chelmsley Wood Police station.

I played a lot of poker with him and a few others and I owed him some money from a game we had played, a couple of weeks previously.

I phoned him from the courts to see if he was at work, and as he was, I told him that I would go over with his money.

I found him in the DI's office and whilst we are having a chat, there was a timid knock on the door and in walked a very *'fresh-faced'* constable, who was on a CID attachment.

Bearing in mind, that here I was, *'suited and booted'* my friend introduced me to him as, Mr....., the new Detective Chief Inspector. He then left me to talk to this lad, whilst he swung round to his desk, pretending to work, and trying not to laugh.

This kid is full of questions and keeps calling me *'Sir'*. He kept asking me what his chances of transferring to the CID were, and what I was looking for in a young detective. I then got his full life and work history and he told me about his best arrests - which didn't amount to much.

He could not have got his nose any further up my *'arse'* if he had tried!

I had to maintain this ruse, whilst my friend was sitting up the corner, trying not to laugh out loud.

This kid then asks me if I would like a cup of coffee.

I said, '*Yes please. Black, two sugars and not too much scotch.*' This was one of my silly, *'throw-away'* lines that I used to say quite often.

The kid then spun on his heels and said, '*I don't think that we have got any whisky, would you like me to go and buy you a bottle?*'

I said, '*Yes, that would be nice.*'

At that point my friend lost it and I left the building."

'Handling it'

"I was the Detective Inspector at Digbeth, and one day I was in my office when I was contacted by a DC and informed that a body had been found at a certain location and that I was required to attend.

My office door was closed and as I turned the knob to open it nothing happened – it just revolved in my hand.

I tried a couple of times with the same result. I telephoned the main CID office to seek assistance from one of my staff but there was no reply.

Eventually I was obliged to contact Steelhouse Lane to ask for assistance.

About ten minutes later the very same DC, (who had also been involved in the Chow Mein incident), turned up at my door with a big grin on his face, and opened it from the outside.

On examination I found that someone had removed the central bar which opened the door…. I never resolved the identity of the culprit but had a good idea.

On another occasion I was called to attend a found body and grabbed my coat as I left the office. As I was moving towards my car I was trying to put my arms in my coat only to find that someone had sewn up the sleeves…..bastards!"

'Going the extra mile'

"Whilst dealing with an insurance fraud on the Stolen Vehicle Squad, together with a colleague, we found that a Bedford Minibus had been disposed of at a scrap yard and then reported as stolen to claim the insurance.

We found that a man who had originated from Pakistan had brought it from the yard and had exported it by ship to his home country. Obviously a positive identification in terms of the chassis number etc. would have been useful.

My colleague drafted a lengthy *'white report'* addressed to the Detective Chief Inspector outlining the facts and the problem we faced.

The report went to a couple of pages and concluded that the vehicle was currently on a ship off Durban in South Africa. He requested authorisation for us to *'parachute onto the deck of the said ship to confirm the ID of the Minibus'.*

The D.C.I. had been engrossed in the report up until that point but was then heard to shout loudly for my colleague to get into his office!"

'In the pink'

"In approximately 1972, the *'pink'* Police Orders, (these were a regular communication detailing personnel moves, promotions, retirements etc), were delivered to all CID officers on the old *'F'* Division. It included an entry showing that a certain detective from Edward Road was being transferred to the Special Patrol Group.

When the DC came on duty at 6pm, on a split shift, that day he saw the Order and went mad.

He phoned up to try to speak to the DCI but he was off duty, and a very sympathetic Detective Sergeant took him and all the CID staff for a curry which he paid for.

The police order was in fact a fake, but the DC only discovered this after *'bending the DCI's ear'* for ten minutes the following morning!"

'Poundland'

"When we were interviewing suspects we sometimes liked to play a game of trying get a random word or saying in if we had the opportunity.

I remember one interview at Bloxwich where a young lad was in possession of cannabis. He worked at *'Poundland'* and whilst searching his bedroom we uncovered ninety-one Halloween ties which, when pressed, made a *'ghostly'* noise.

Well, on interview I had to get this one in and said, *'How much would they sell for then at Poundland?'*

He looked at me for about a minute and then said, *'I think they are a pound.'*

Well what a surprise!"

'A 'Bluenose' tail'

"There was a difference between the CID at Digbeth, who often dressed down and used backstreet pubs, and the CID at Steelhouse Lane, who always wore suits and a tie, and frequented the nightclubs.

One common factor however, was the constant *'banter'* that took place amongst the staff. For instance, one of the Detective Sergeants managed to get hold of an old Director's chair from the wholesale markets, in which he occasionally used to doze during the afternoons.

Someone got hold of a pig's tail from a butcher and pinned it underneath the chair. After about a week the Sergeant started contacting the estates department to complain about the number of flies appearing in the office. He was also perturbed by a strange smell that prevailed.

Eventually he was put out of his misery and someone told him that it was there. He went ballistic and tried to complain to the Chief Inspector who took no notice of him.

They were not the best of friends and on another occasion the Sergeant was given a warning about not attending the matches at Birmingham City in duty time, under threat of being removed from the CID.

He was a big *'Bluenose'* and despite this he carried on going.

Then one Sunday the *'Mercury'* newspaper published an article about the match, together with a photograph of one of the goalmouths. Prominently positioned in the photo next to the goalposts was the Detective Sergeant, plain for all to see.

Numerous copies were made and posted around the station and, as fast as the Sergeant removed them, other photocopies were put up!"

'Time Management'

"Whilst I was on the Drug Squad in the early 1990s, we regularly worked very long hours, sometimes in excess of sixty hours per week.

They didn't have a budget to pay all of our overtime so on occasions we were allowed a *'Poets Day'*, (Piss Off Early Tomorrow's Saturday), where we could finish a bit earlier provided everything had been done.

We frequently did this on a Friday afternoon, when the practice was to finish duty after we had been to the courts to apply for search warrants, which we would execute the following week.

We would type the paperwork out and then take it to the Magistrates Clerk's Offices where it was checked before we were allocated a court.

On Friday afternoons the Magistrates had normally finished their normal day's business and the Magistrates and a Magistrate's Clerk would be waiting in a rear office for you.

Normally an application for a search warrant would take about fifteen to twenty minutes as officers took the oath, made the application, and then answered any questions from the magistrates.

One particular Friday I booked out to apply for a warrant but was surprised when I arrived to find a number of other crews there with eight applications ready to go in just one court.

We were last in the queue and as time passed it was apparent that the time spent for each application had reduced from twenty minutes to ten minutes. It appeared that the Magistrates and the Clerk all had urgent appointments to get to and were under some pressure to conclude proceedings.

At the time I was in the company of another very experienced officer who told me to leave things with him as we were finally ushered inside the court.

As he took the oath, the conversation then went something along the lines of,

'Afternoon your worships. I swear by almighty God that the evidence I will give shall be the truth, the whole truth, and nothing but the truth... I understand that you are in somewhat of a hurry.'

One of the magistrates responded, *'Yes we are already late.'*

The officer replied, *'Then I will be brief. The application relates to ......address and a man by the name of....... He's done it before and he's at it again.'*

The application took just two minutes and the warrant was signed – something of a record!"

'That's a new one on me'

"An elderly lady was *'nicked'* by the CID at Bloxwich on suspicion of fraud. Basically, she was looking after youth players for one of the big clubs and was making applications for credit cards in one particular player's name.

Whilst being questioned by a certain officer she *'piped up'*, *'Well I was robbing Peter to pay Paul.'*

At this the officer said, *'Well, you never mentioned these two before, who are they?'*

From the Detective Sergeant, who was in the interview, there was a deathly silence!"

'A special request'

"On a Birmingham inner-city Sub-Division, we had a big bobby who was a body builder/powerlifter and liked everyone to know how strong he was. He did all that screaming in the gym type of shit.

One night, the shift decided to play a *'blag'* on him and he was called into his Inspector's office and shown a telex message.

The Inspector informed him that there was going to be a terrorist incident in Birmingham and the *'SAS'* were going to land on Billesley Common between 3am and 4am.

His job was to make a big letter *'H'* with telex paper rolls, on the ground, and to shine two heavy *'dragon lamps'*, (powerful and large hand-held lights), up into the air for an hour.

Needless to say, he was sworn to secrecy by the Inspector.

The officer duly went to the scene to carry out his task but after about ten minutes he was on the radio asking for the Inspector to join him.

The Inspector spoke to him on the radio and the officer said, *'They're too heavy sir. I can't keep this up.'*

The Inspector retorted, *'You're supposed to be strong. That's why I selected you to shine those fucking lamps!'*

Eventually his shift appeared from hiding in the woods nearby to take *'the piss'* and put him out of his misery."

'Look into my eyes'

"In the 90's a new Enquiry Office Assistant started at Darlaston Police Station and two of the response officers convinced her that they could hypnotise people.

She agreed to test their skills and one of the officers sat her down and went through the process of *'hypnotising'* her whilst her eyes were closed.

At the end of his *'speech'* he indicated that when she opened her eyes again, on his command, the second officer would appear to be in the room completely naked.

Unbeknown to her, whilst she had her eyes closed the second officer stripped off and sat on a chair with a large book strategically placed to cover his *'modesty'*.

She duly opened her eyes and completely freaked out, thinking that she was seeing things!"

'A stroll in the park'

"It was in the mid-Eighties and I was on my last set of nights as a Sergeant on response duties at Bournville, before going back into the CID, when my shift and the Control Room staff decided to set me up. My Inspector had already told them that for a number of reasons he didn't think it was a good idea, but the plot was hatched and they went ahead.

Well into the dark hours of the morning, a call came over the radio that there was a stolen moped in one of the parks and I made my way there where I found one of the dog handlers *'hunkered down'*. We could hear a moped roaring round.

A stream ran through the park and railway
sleepers had been placed across it in different places
so that people could cross.

Suddenly one of my *'Panda'* crews turned up
on the other side of the park and started chasing the
moped. The rider abandoned it and ran off pursued by
officers in the rain.

Just the previous night I had found a stolen car
with *'two up'*, (two people on board), doing
'wheelies' around the same area and so I was very
familiar with the layout. I had managed to
successfully cordon off the area in Kings Norton with
officers and after they abandoned the vehicle, which
hit a house, I eventually managed to arrest the two
single-handed and lead them into custody handcuffed
together.

I enjoyed telling the story on the night so it
was perhaps no surprise that this was the subject of
the *'blag'*.

Anyway, back to the story. I stealthily ditched
my raincoat, jacket etc. in preparation for the
anticipated chase, and then when the time was right, I
moved to bring down the *'gazelle'* that was being
pursued, who appeared to be 6' 4" tall, built like a
'brick shithouse' and wearing a crash-helmet.

As I went to intercept him, he saw me and
stopped running on the opposite side of the stream.
There was pandemonium going on with lots of
shouting.

I'm still at full-pelt with the music of
'Chariots of Fire' ringing in my ears, and I decided a
drop-kick was what was needed and launched myself
at him just as I reached the wet sleepers. I went right
down and initially slid right past him before hauling
myself back up to tackle him.

By now he had moved to a wider and deeper stretch of the stream and as I grappled with him, we both fell into the water. I was immediately thinking *'weapons'*, so at this stage I was on top and I pulled his crash-helmet off to reveal a balaclava.

We continued rolling around in the water and I was screaming, *'I've got him'* as his crash-helmet floated downstream. Then a number of other officers dived in and grabbed me and I was thinking *'medals all round'* for this one, until the *'prisoner'* started spluttering *'He's fucking mad',* and it slowly dawned on me that it was the voice of one of the shift.

One female officer was on the far bank laughing so hard I got annoyed. She stopped laughing after she fell into the water…..

Back at the *'nick'* the control staff and all of my shift came out and clapped as the *'soaking wet'* team came in. The Inspector stood there shaking his head with that *'told you so'* look on his face.

I never did get a medal!"

'Another 'April Fool''

"In 1981 as a young Sergeant at Aston, I had just qualified as a firearms officer. Needless to say, I let everyone know. The date was March 31st and we had just started night duty.

I was the Station Sergeant that night, and at about 11.30pm the Controller told me that there was a firearms incident happening and that *'firearms officers'* were to standby.

To say I was excited and scared in equal measures was an understatement, and I even spoke to the Force Control Room who confirmed that the incident was taking place and to await a telex message for further instructions.

A very tense few minutes later at 0005hrs the telex machine started up. I waited with my heart in my mouth as the message came up, *'APRIL FOOL'*.

There was much laughter from the Controller's office next door – bastards!"

'Watch out there's a dog about'

"Whilst I was being 'tutored', we had a call one Christmas Day when I was on nights to go to some factory units in Darlaston where an alarm had gone off. Because of the time of day, we thought it might be genuine, so a thorough search took place over a period of more than twenty minutes.

Whilst this was going on, I climbed onto the roof and lay down watching the other officers searching below.

We didn't find anyone but after a while my tutor constable noticed I was missing and started calling my name out. As he started to climb towards the roof I started *'barking'* at him – he nearly had a heart attack!

In those days it wasn't unusual for officers to start *'barking'* especially if chasing suspects. The shout would go up, *'stop or I will let the dog go!'* followed by a good impression of a German Shepherd."

(This ruse was regularly used across the West Midlands Police Force, and had a good deal of success, proportionate to one's skill in impersonating a large German Shepherd dog. If you sounded like an excitable Jack Russell it had a lot less effect).

'Déjà vu in Digbeth'

"I think the best *'blag'* I ever played was on my Inspector at Digbeth.

Routinely, when working nights, one of the Panda drivers, at about 4am, would do the 'paper run' and go to Mapstones, (the main newspaper distributor for the whole of Birmingham), in Wrentham Street, just off Ladywell Walk, and collect the papers for the nick. They would give us two of each newspaper that was printed and my Inspector always had the *'Birmingham Post'*.

This one particular night I asked the Mapstone's night manager, if there were any *'Birmingham Post's'* left from the night before.

He found one for me, and with the rest of the papers I duly set off for the *'nick'*, but not before taking the cover pages off today's and yesterday's *'Birmingham Post'* and putting the complete inner pages from yesterday's *'Birmingham Post'* inside the outer pages of that days *'Birmingham Post'*.

I delivered the papers to Digbeth Front Office, and then took the 'doctored' *'Birmingham Post'* into the Inspector's office. As was the norm I asked him if he wanted a cup of coffee. I then went to the controller's office and told the controller I was making the *'gaffer'* a cup of coffee. This I did and took it back into him.

As I turned to walk out, he said, *'Have you ever experienced Déjà vu?'* Looking as though I didn't understand what he was talking about I turned to him and said, *'Don't know what you mean gaffer.'* He replied, *'When you see or do something that you think you've done exactly the same before but you haven't.'* I said, *'Yeah, yeah, I know what you mean. Yes, gaffer I have.'* He replied, *'I keep thinking I've read all these stories before.'*

I left his office, and fell about laughing my head off."

'The Royal visit'

"We did a fake telex message at Bradford Street police station once, which read that Prince Charles was landing in a helicopter in the *'SPG'* (Special Patrol Group), yard. One officer spent frantic hours trying to trace the owners of all the cars parked out there so that he could get them moved to make room."

'A word from the 'big boss''

"When I was an Inspector at on a certain Birmingham Sub-Division the elusiveness and invisibility of the then Chief Superintendent to the lower ranks was legendary. There were people who had worked there for years and didn't know what he looked like, let alone ever meeting him.

We were chatting about this as a group one day, when one of the shift 'wags' announced that he had met the man once.

We listened, enraptured, as the officer described being posted to the cordon for a Royal visit. He knew that the Chief Superintendent would be there, escorting the Royal visitors, and wondered whether he might catch a glimpse, perhaps even exchange pleasantries with the 'big boss'.

Sure enough, as the party of dignitaries approached, a figure bearing the 'Crown and Bath Star', (Chief Superintendent's insignia) parted from the group and approached our boy who thought, 'this is it, he's recognised me after all these years and is taking the opportunity to pass a few words'.

The 'big boss' approached, our boy gave a salute and an, *'All Correct Sir'*. The Chief Superintendent responded, *'move that fucking cone.'*"

'A tall story'

"I used to work with a bobby on the 'J' Division. He was a good officer, and when he puffed his chest out and stretched to his full height, he was all of 5'5" to 5'6" tall. (Remember there were height restrictions on recruits until relatively recently, so shorter male officers were for or a long time, a rarity).

One day I was reading on the Force intranet a message from the Press Office at Lloyd House.

The message read something like, *'We have been contacted by a television production company who are looking for Britain's tallest police officer. They are particularly looking for an officer in uniform, and in return for a day of the officer's time they will donate five hundred pounds to a charity of choice. Do we have any tall officers in the West Midlands?'*

I rang the Press Office and spoke to a media officer, introducing myself as being the short officer, and that I had just read the message. The conversation went along the following lines:

The media officer, *'Oh yes. How tall are you?'*

Me, *'I'm six feet eleven inches tall.'*

The media officer, *'Oh my word. I've had a couple of 6'8" tall officers on the phone, but you are the tallest so far. There was a 'bobby' in the 'Met' who was 7'1" tall, a basket-ball player, but I heard that he has retired.'*

I said, *'I'm a bit self-conscious about my height and I wouldn't normally get involved in this sort of thing but the donation to charity has swung it.'*

The media person confirmed that I was a uniformed officer and then said that they would get back to me.

A few days later the short officer's Inspector was contacted by the Press Office asking that he be made available for a day's filming with the television production company, because they thought that he was Britain's tallest police officer.

The Inspector clarified what it was for and concluded, *'He's five feet 'fucking' nothing and he's the shortest officer on the Division – it's someone 'blagging' you.'"*

'The ring of fire'

"One of our colleagues on the OSU, (Operational Support Unit), came to Thornhill Road on promotion as a Sergeant, where a certain Greek Cypriot fish and chip shop was used by the *'troops'*.

If we were free our new Sergeant would ask us to bring him some chips and a kebab with not too much chilli sauce in it.

Over a period of time on a few second-watch, (2pm – 10pm), shifts, we started gradually increasing the quantity of chilli sauce on his kebab. The chip shop owner's son was up for the *'blag'* and continually asked us how much to put on.

The Sergeant would never admit that it was too hot for him and would suffer in silence and sweat profusely as he worked his way through each one.

Eventually even the owner's son got squeamish about the amount of chilli sauce he was putting on but nothing was ever said – those OSU officers were tough!"

'The skeleton key'

"It was about 19.45 hours on a dark weekday evening, when we received a call that there was an intruder alarm activation at the Trustees Savings Bank offices, in Lionel Street, City Centre.
It was not a bank, just a four-storey office block for TSB.

I was driving *'FZ1'*, (fast response car), with another officer, but we were some distance away.

Another officer who was single-manned in *'FM1'*, (panda car), and slightly closer, radioed up and said that he would also make towards it as well.

Both cars arrived at the same time. We found that one of the main front doors was wide open and an elderly gentleman was just inside the foyer with a postal sack, putting a number of parcels and letters into it.

We could also hear a faint audible alarm ringing inside the building, but there was nothing audible outside.

The other two officers went upstairs to trace the source of the alarm, whilst I checked the man with the postal sack, who was claiming to be a courier for TSB, his job being to collect all of the post and parcels from the various offices and banks in Birmingham and take them to a central distribution point.

He had all the correct photo identification and claimed that the alarm was ringing when he arrived. He had only arrived seconds before we did. He was no trace on *'PNC'*, (Police National Computer), and a few other checks found him to be exactly who he claimed to be.

I asked him how he got into the building, and he produced a sheet of paper with the door access codes for all of the TSB offices and banks on it.

I then noticed that the front door had a push-button entry system, identical to the systems found outside every police station cell block. The number for this office block was a four-digit number which I memorized.

After the courier left, I went upstairs to look for the other two. I could hear the alarm sounding within a 1st floor office, but there was no trace of my colleagues.

Outside this office was another of these push button entry systems......I wondered if it had the same code throughout the whole building and inserted the four numbers – yes it did!

At that point I could hear voices coming down the stairs.

I quickly shut the office door, and re-entered the code again, so that the door was unlocked, but not open. I took out my bank-card and as soon as I was aware that my colleagues were behind me, I pretended to slip this security lock with my card and opened the door.

What I didn't realise, was that they had found a Regional Manager for TSB, working in his office on the top floor, who was completely oblivious to the fact that his alarm was going off. To be fetched out of his office by two of the *'West Midlands finest'* and then to find me on my knees, slipping his bank security lock with my 'Barclays' bank card didn't improve his mood.

Needless to say, he was not impressed, especially when he examined the alarm panel and it displayed – *'1st floor office door tamper'*!

As everything was in order, we left the Regional Manager to await the Alarm Company and we hurried down the stairs.

At this point the single-crewed officer said to me, *'How the fuck did you manage to open that door with your bank card?'*

I said, *'It's easy, you just need to line up the magnetic strip on your card with the lock mechanism and then enter your bank PIN number.'*

He said, *'Bollocks – if that works, then show me on the main entry door.'*

All three of us then stood outside the offices and my inquisitive colleague confirmed to his satisfaction that the main door was well and truly locked. Bank card in hand, magnetic strip lined up, I entered the four numbers, telling the officer that was my PIN number. The door was now open!

My other colleague obviously realized what had just happened and proceeded to go along with it, telling him that he had seen me open the cell-block doors at both Steelhouse Lane, and Digbeth, using the same method.

We then left the scene and I told the colleague I was partnered-up with the story, and how I had managed to open the doors.

Unknown to us the other officer headed straight to Digbeth Police station and started messing about with his own bank-card, and the security lock into the custody block, much to the amusement of the front office civilian, because of course he couldn't open the door....strange that!

A similar attempt was then made at *'The Lane'*, (Steelhouse Lane), that failed again.

He put a call in via the Control Room –
'Foxtrot Zulu one, what is your location for Foxtrot Mike one to meet up?'

We met and he said, *"I've tried my card at 'The Lane' and Digbeth, and it doesn't work."*

I said, *'It might not, if you are overdrawn.'*

He paused and said, *'Actually, I am. That's probably why then.'*

A few days later, after payday, when there was money in his account, guess who was still trying to open cell-block doors with his bank card?

Exasperated, he said to me at some point, *'Show me again how to do it.'*

I lined up my magnetic strip and then entered the actual code for the cell-block...which he failed to notice and the door opened.

He said, *'Well my card doesn't work.'*

I said, *'If I were you, I would contact your bank.'*

Did I say, one of *'West Midland's finest.'"*

'The Indian rope trick'

"I was stationed in the Black Country as a young PC, and having my yearly appraisal with my shift Inspector. He was an old-style boss, very set in his ways, nobody was granted leave when on night duty, and you had to play him at snooker when you were on your meal break if he found you…consequently we hid away from him much of the time.

At my appraisal time, we were sat in an office which faced the front of the building, and had large high windows. Staff appraisals were pretty much a waste of time back then, but had to be done because well…they just had to be done. The Inspector had his back to the window and I was sat facing it. Whilst sat there listening to him tell me how I should be applying and studying for my promotion exams, I suddenly saw a very thick rope drop down outside the window, the sort of thing that you would see in a school gym.

I sat there wondering what was going to happen next and slightly bemused. Then slowly, inch by inch, a pair of feet appeared then went back up out of sight. The Inspector carried on completely oblivious to the whole situation telling me how I should *'do this and do that.'*

Next, as equally slowly as before, a head suddenly appeared, followed by the rest of the body, again inch by inch, working down the rope. I could hardly contain myself.

The person disappeared all the way down past the window and then the rope just fell at which point the Inspector asked me whether there was anything I wanted to add. I was on the point of bursting out laughing at this point and just about contained myself before saying, *'no.'*

When I walked into the front office downstairs there were the culprits smiling and obviously chuffed at their exploits – their own version of the 'Indian rope trick.'"

'Cowboy's & Indians'

"In the 1990s, the police were called to a house in Birmingham by an Indian householder stating that he had killed a man. He had engaged a builder to do a loft conversion but he was a night worker and had asked the builder to come after dinner times, (that's lunchtime in Birmingham), so that he could get some sleep. The builder used it as an excuse not to go very often which led to a dispute and threats of legal action. As a result, the builder then deliberately started going early and kept waking up the householder.

One morning the builder was making a lot of noise and the householder snapped, went into the loft and hit the builder over the head with a lump hammer killing him instantly.

Police attended together with SOCO, (Scenes Of Crime Officers), and the person was arrested.

Later on, a Detective Chief Inspector was holding a briefing and allocating actions when he said to a Detective Sergeant, *'Sarge make some enquiries to see if the builder was a 'cowboy' builder.'*

The Sergeant said, *'Sir. I don't think I need to do that – it's obvious he was a cowboy, – he was killed by the Indian.'*

The room collapsed in laughter at a very tense time. Much humour in the job comes from tragedy, so at times can be very dark."

'Spinning & yet more spinning'

Spinning was another 'dark art'. It was a speciality of the Operational Support Units, and no doubt totally bemusing to an outsider. It comprised causing a person to turn around, that's pretty much it! Using a person's name was not allowed, but apart from that, pretty much anything went.

As a senior officer, it was common, when passing parked-up OSU vans, to 'run a gauntlet' of coughs, window-taps and *'Excuse Me's',* and one had to hold one's neck in a forward-looking vice to prevent any assumption that one had been *'spun'*, and provoking cheers and laughter.....

"During the Miner's Strike I managed to *'spin'* the South Yorkshire Chief Constable and his Deputy. Also, one lad got taken ill, (probably from an overdose of pork-pies), and was being stretchered out of the gymnasium-come dormitory by two ambulance-men. They got *'spun'* and dropped the police officer who was ill off the stretcher, as they suddenly turned around.

It got to the stage when no-one would turn around to an arbitrary shout, or a dropped coin, which could count as a *'spin'*. Calling a person by name was not 'allowed'.

Eventually the term, *'official no blag'*, had to prefix any genuine requests to gain someone's attention."

'Barking mad'

"I was a young *'Pro-Con'* with about 12 months service when I got mobilised from my bed to go to Handsworth on the occasion of the riots. I had of course been subject to *'blags'* and *'spins'* but I was about to witness a masterly combination of both, in the most stressful of situations.

It was the early hours of the morning after the riots began, that I found myself in a van full of bleary-eyed officers, arriving in the back yard of Thornhill Road Police Station. En- route we had driven down Lozells Road, which looked like it had been bombed, and we knew that people had been killed there a few hours previously. I had never experienced anything like this and it felt like I was going to war, so I was nervous, and I suspect I was not alone.

Things had quietened down a little, so we were fresh officers, being held in reserve, awaiting deployment if trouble erupted again. On arrival we were fed, which was standard procedure, and then left to basically 'hang about' until we were required.

Everyone was in full 'riot gear', which included thick, flame-retardant boiler suits over our uniforms, and heavy 'public order' boots. It was high summer and boiling hot, so everybody naturally gravitated outside and into the back yard.

The yard was pretty full of vehicles, and there was a row of 'dog vans' parked on the left-hand side of the yard. Because of the heat, their rear doors were wide open, the dogs confined by the internal grille doors. Police dogs are well-trained, but if one barks, then, like most dogs, the others will start as well.

Hidden behind the vans, leaning against the building, was sat and sprawled, a large number of tired, bored and I think, 'nervy' officers, a classic police environment for tension-breaking humour.

Suddenly, the officer in charge of Handsworth Sub-Division appeared from the other side of the yard, accompanied by a gaggle of media people. We all watched with interest as cameras were set up, using the row of dog vans as an impressive background. Clearly an interview for the morning BBC News was about to take place.

Neither the senior officer, nor the media people, could see the officers sat behind the vans. I was sat further down the line and could see both the media gaggle and the resting officers.

A good deal of time was spent setting up for the interview, and then the great moment came.

The reporter lifted the microphone and asked the first question. Before the senior officer could reply, the yard was filled with a hellish cacophony as one dog barked and then the rest joined in. *'Cut'*.

The interview was reset. The dogs quietened down. The first question was asked…and, as if on cue, the dogs began barking again.

This incredible bad luck continued several times, until the senior officer lost it and began yelling, 'shut those fucking dogs up.' Eventually, having failed in this endeavour, the interview was moved to somewhere more peaceful.

Of course, every time the interview began, an officer having both sightlines gave a signal, and another 'wag' hidden behind the vans, kicked one, causing the dog inside to bark, and the subsequent chain-reaction.

This cheered everyone up immensely and put me in a good frame of mind to cope with being petrol-bombed later on!"

'Has anyone seen...'

"Every cop knows who the biggest *'blaggers'* as a team were, the Operational Support Unit, or OSU.

They were brilliantly professional but spent a lot of time sat in vans waiting to do things and I guess the boredom spawned a multitude of *'blags'*, until it became their main occupation when not engaged operationally. They were competitive too, in trying to outdo each other with bigger and better *'blags'*.

Sometimes they went too far, and got their wrists slapped, but I couldn't help but admire their endless ingenuity and found great amusement in their antics, often where I shouldn't have, and it was often childish – but you had to be there.

One day on early shift I went down to take my breakfast *'refs'* in the canteen at Steelhouse Lane. This canteen was very large and very popular, not just with those working at *'The Lane'*, but with officers at court and visiting Birmingham. In this occasion it was packed, and several van-loads of OSU were in for breakfast.

Some of the canteen staff had been there for years and knew just about everyone. They were brilliant at their job but because it was so busy, didn't have time for chit-chat and tended to run breakfast along military lines.

One in particular was extremely well-liked but renowned for not standing any nonsense, and many an officer of any rank had had a dose of the sharp side of her tongue, and she had a booming voice that was instantly recognisable.

She had a good sense of humour, you had to have when dealing with us lot, but this morning was the *'blag'* where she snapped, and of course it was the OSU that did it.

It was the simplest of *'blags'* really. The canteen had a tannoy system which was also routed throughout the building. This was essential because often officers on *'refs'* had to be called to court or other duties and *'scrambled'* from eating.
The lady in question was usually the one to operate the tannoy, I suspect this was considered a 'serious' task and she had claimed it as a mark of seniority amongst the canteen staff.

A member of the OSU had clearly handed her a message.......

I nearly choked on my breakfast when she suddenly bellowed through the tannoy,

'Telephone call for Mike Hunt.'

There was a silence as scores of munching jaws stopped, unsure of what they had just heard.

'There's a telephone call for Mike Hunt.'

Pennies were beginning to drop.

'Has anybody seen Mike Hunt?'

It went on and on, with variations, and each one provoked increasing gales of laughter. The lady in question looked increasingly angry and puzzled until someone finally took pity and explained the laughter.

I believe that she marched straight up to the Superintendent's office and complained, and some punishment for the perpetrator(s) followed."

'Negotiation masterclass'

"A Sergeant was called to Junction 10 of the M6, following a report that an obese man had climbed over the railings of the elevated intersection, and was threatening to jump onto the motorway below into the path of oncoming motorway traffic.

Initially the man refused to allow the officer to approach him but he *'dug deep'* into all the reasons as to why he thought the man shouldn't end his life in this way.

After about twenty minutes the suicidal man showed all the signs of starting to heed the officer's words of wisdom.

Just at that moment however, all of the officer's hard work was undone in a split second when passengers in a builder's van travelling around the motorway island shouted,

'Jump ya fat bastard.'

Back to square one!

'The old biker'

"I doctored my Advanced motorbike course joining instructions, adding in the name of one of the Sergeants who looked after the Permanent Beat Officers on our Sub-Division. We then sat in the office listening to him on the phone to the driving school, getting more irate with whoever he was talking to by the minute. He kept telling them that he had the joining instructions in front of him and that there must be a mistake.

He was looking round at us and at that point we just couldn't keep straight faces!

He suggested I didn't have a father but then took it in good part."

'Sweet FA'

"Circa 2009 I was working with a PCSO, (Police Community Support Officer), at Lye who was a very good footballer and decided to organise a football tournament for local kids. His mum was a senior member of Police Staff at Lloyd House Headquarters with good connections to the senior officers.

The PCSO wrote to all the local clubs, Birmingham City, Villa, the Albion, Wolves, and requested *'freebies'* to give away as prizes.

He also wrote to the Football Association.

A few weeks later I overheard him saying that the clubs had sent things but the FA hadn't.

That afternoon I slipped a piece of paper on his desk saying, *'Can you ring Scott Lee on* (external number for the Chief Constables Secretary*). He's from the FA, something to do with your football tournament.'* The conversation went something like this…

PA, 'Senior Officers Secretary.'

Him, *'Hello my name is ………from the West Midlands Police. May I speak to Scott Lee please?'*

PA, *'Yes. What is it you want to speak to him about?'*

Him, *'I'm organising a football tournament for local kids and I think he's got some stuff for me to give away as prizes.'*

PA, *'How do you know this?'*

Him, *'He has left a message for me to contact him.'*

PA, *'And it's Paul Scott Lee, the Chief Constable, that you wish to talk to?'*

The PCSO looked at my note as I was watching him from the other side of the room and concluded, *'Can I ring you back please?'*

His mum later heard that her son had been introduced to the delights of *'blagging'."*

'A certain something about him'

"When I was at a public meeting a little old lady looked at me adoringly and said, *'Sergeant X, you have 'Charisma' with a capital 'C'.'*

I replied, *'It's funny you should say that. I've been called lots of things with a capital 'C'.'*

The room erupted with laughter – at least half of it did.

The *'less worldly'* looked bemused, but luckily my words did not deter the old girl. Never underestimate an old lady."

'Bali Hai'

"Following a spate of robberies in Birmingham City Centre during the late Seventies, I decided to set up an operation using various static observation points in office blocks overlooking the streets, as well as having officers on the ground in plain clothes to act as arrest teams.

One relatively new probationer was included in the teams to get experience, and the day before the operation he consulted colleagues as to what he should wear.

He was informed that it was most important that he didn't look anything like a police officer and therefore dressing as if he was a tourist would work well.

Next day he duly turned up for the briefing wearing a bright *'Hawaiian'* multi-coloured shirt that you would be able to spot from several miles away. He was duly assigned to one of the inside observation points. His opportunity for glory lost!"

'Miami Vice'

"This has to be the best *'blag'*, I was ever involved in/instigated.

It would have been in about 1986, I was working on the Divisional Support Unit with a Sergeant and a number of other officers.

In the office next door was the Divisional Observations Team – known as the *'DOTS'*.

'Miami Vice' was a big hit on the television at the time and one of my team, being a little on the naïve side, was highly influenced by it, even resorting to pushing up the sleeves on his jacket and talking in a phony American accent.

He would often talk about how he would love to go to Florida and I advised him to look out for temporary transfers to police forces in other countries.

I left it a few months and with the assistance of our Sergeant, we managed to get hold of some Headquarters Memorandum paper – which was yellow at the time.

We then wrote a police-exchange report with officers from *'Dade County Police'*, in Florida.

Rather than just have one post, we decided to write it for five posts; as we thought that the officer might see through it, so we created roles for a Superintendent, an Inspector, a Detective Sergeant and two Constable posts.

One of the Constable posts came with a heavy traffic bias, and the other for a plain clothes/undercover type of officer.

Although naïve, my colleague held some very good educational qualifications, all of which he needed for this particular post – funny that!

It would be a minimum attachment of two years, with two paid return flights to the UK per year, and with firearms training to be given by Dade County. There would be a brief initial conversion course, which, after completion, would give successful applicants full USA Police powers!

It took us over a week to write this report, bearing in mind we had to compose the other rank's requirements.

We also needed a point of contact – but my Sergeant had a friend who was an Inspector at Lloyd House, Force Headquarters, who was something to do with recruiting. He allowed us to use his contact details, through whom all applications would need to go.

Needless to say, all of the other officers on our two little squads were in on this.

The memo was printed off and left on a desk in our office......for our unsuspecting victim to find!

See if you can guess what happened next? Yes, he did!

'*What have you got there*?' He was asked one day by one of our team.

He was very reluctant to show us his application form, but eventually did; prompting one of the *'DOTS'* officers to say that he was going to apply for the same Constable's post.

The officer now had a rival, who had not got the required qualifications that he had, and he took great pleasure in pointing that out to his colleague.

Undeterred, the other officer maintained the *'blag'* and told him that he was still going to submit an application.

Eventually I was asked by the victim, '.... *you're good at wording applications, can you give me a hand to write my application*?' So.. I did.

An application was expertly written and glowingly endorsed by the Sergeant who also endorsed the application from the second officer who was in on it. He didn't give him such a strong reference though.

The applications were submitted to the Inspector at HQ, preceded by a phone call as what he could expect to receive.

During the following weeks, as the application deadline approached, we convinced our hapless victim that he was going to be the successful candidate and encouraged him to keep phoning the friendly Inspector, to see how his application was progressing.

Our victim was duly informed that the Inspector in recruiting had only received two applications, namely his own and the one from the second officer. He was even told, *'between you and me, the other officer will not make it through the paper-sift.'*

He was a very happy man, and unknown to us at the time, was trying to sell his car to raise extra money, as he would not need it for at least the next two years, and had also withdrawn an offer he had put in on a house he was interested in buying!

The next stage of his *'application'*, was a pre-assessment suitability interview with the Divisional Superintendent.

The Superintendent was updated on the *'blag'* and agreed to interview the officer in his office. His intention was to tape-record it and then to reveal to him that it was all an elaborate hoax.

One very *'up-beat'* officer duly left our office one day and was last seen heading towards the Divisional Supt's office.

After about forty-five minutes, a laughing Superintendent came into our office, with Dictaphone in hand and began to play us the recording:

Supt: *'How do you get on with the rest of your colleagues?'*

Officer: *'Great bunch of lads, they have been very supportive.'*

Supt: *'I always got the impression that you were the butt of their jokes.'*

Officer: *'Yes, well, I used to be, but they have left me alone recently.'*

Supt: *'What would you say, if I told you that this application was just an elaborate hoax?'*

Officer, after a long silence: *'You fucking bastard.'*

Laughing Superintendent in the background, followed by the sound of a chair being kicked over and a slamming door!

At this point, we realized that we had not seen the officer since he had left our office en route to his bogus interview; he hadn't come back. He had left the Superintendent's office about fifteen minutes before the Superintendent had come down to us to play the tape......Oh, shit, we've lost him.....we need to find him !!!

He was eventually found in the bar of the *'Queens Head'*, having consumed several large scotches and a couple of pints.

He was no longer up-beat.

We tried to placate him, *'Come on X, we are really sorry, no, honest we are. Please come back and we will take you down the bar at 'The Lane', we'll buy your beer all night and take you for a curry afterwards.'*

This plea was met with a torrent of abuse, which was understandable and justified; especially after somebody asked him if he was still thinking of selling his car...there was no need for that!

He came back to Steelhouse Lane bar after the licensee of the *'Queens Head'* asked him to leave for excessive swearing, and we proceeded to get him very drunk.

It was now about 6pm and the bar was starting to fill with the regulars, one of which was the Detective Inspector. He wanted to know what the *'Craic'* was, so he was told about the police-exchange *'blag'*.

The D.I. thought it was brilliant and asked to have a look at the report. My Sergeant agreed to leave a copy on his desk before he went home.

I later found out that the night-turn Detective Sergeant at *'The Lane'*, had rummaged through the D.I's office, (a regular night-time 'intelligence-gathering' occupation), came across the *'blag'* report, and applied for the D.S's post.

A *'double-blag!'*"

'Loose change'

"In the late 1970's, whilst working with an observations team who had been deployed to keep an eye out for armed robbers attacking security vehicles in Colmore Row, Birmingham City-Centre, I had occasion to visit one of the observations points. Whilst I was there, I was surprised to find that in the street below people kept bending down trying to pick something up off the floor. Some would walk past and then return to the spot whilst others made sweeping arm movements as they tried to pick the object up without breaking their stride.

Men in pin-stripe suits, well-dressed women, students, and all manner of society made valiant attempts but failed.

When I went back to street-level I discovered that a coin had been superglued to the floor. I looked up towards the observations point and could swear that I could just make out someone with a big grin on his face!

Another retired officer also recalls that this became a favourite pastime in police offices where coins were glued to tiled floors and occasionally boot polish was put around the rim of telephone handsets resulting in a ring of black around the call recipient's ear."

'This job's a piece of piss'

"On the Drug Squad we would undertake our own surveillance.

One such operation had me as the cameraman in Moseley Street, Balsall Heath. My job was to film a crack cocaine transaction as part of the evidence gathering process. The transaction would take place outside the *'Moseley Arms'*. At that time, right opposite the pub was a small public car park, and on the corner of that car park, roadside, was a large mature rhododendron bush. It was perfect for me to settle down into in the darkness and to get a view of the pub and film at the same time.

It was November, and freezing. The deal was to take place at 7pm and I got into position at about 6pm and settled down. I could hear the surveillance team on my earpiece and everything was going to plan. At about 6.45pm the buyer turned up in his vehicle and parked on the car park. I filmed him arriving and got the registration plate – all was going well.

At 7pm the seller pulled up outside the pub. I had filmed his arrival – Martin Scorsese eat your heart out!

I could hear the buyer get out of his car and begin to walk towards the seller's car. Just then I became aware of the sound of a verse from my childhood being sung nearby, an Irish Republican song called *'Kevin Barry'*. I could see *'Paddy'* with his bottle of *'Thunderbird'* wine come staggering towards my bush.

'Kevin Barry gave up his young life for the cause of liberty' rang out in my head as he stood right in front of me, undid his flies and *'pissed'* all over me, and my very expensive digital camera.

By the time he had shaken his member, zipped up his flies, and staggered off, the transaction had taken place and the seller was driving away.

In my ears was the team leader, *'did you get the transaction?'*

I replied, *'Not really, I need a shower.'"*

'A day out in Stratford'

"One of the jobs I was involved in related to a team of *'ram-raiders'* who were operating in the Midlands.

One day we had them under observations in a stolen Ford Sierra Cosworth as they drove to Stratford Upon Avon and rammed the front door of an independent clothes shop.

The *'troops'* closed in, and the criminals jumped into the Cosworth and tried to escape down an alley, only to be cut off by an officer driving a brand-new Cavalier – who would give way first?

The answer was neither, as the two cars merged into a pile of oily, smoky junk and demolished the porch of a nearby building of historical value.

With police officers swarming all over the place the team battled with the *'ram-raiders'* in an effort to arrest them.

In those days we were armed with just pickaxe handles and bamboo sticks.

During the course of the violent struggle, one of the criminals received a blow to the head which required him being taken to hospital, and rumours later abounded that he had a fractured skull.

In the middle of all this, I distinctly remember the senior officer present puffing on his cigar, and posing for photographs among the wreckage, for a group of Japanese tourists who were visiting Stratford for the day, whilst he extolled the virtues of the Vauxhall Cavalier car.

We subsequently received a letter from the local police asking if we could arrest such criminals either before or after they had committed offences as it was far too expensive to sort the mess out afterwards.

The *'blag'* came when someone created a false telex message afterwards requesting that the clothing of the officer who had struck the prisoner be seized for forensic purposes, together with his car and weapons, as the person concerned was deceased and that a criminal investigation was underway.

As you can imagine the officer went ballistic until he realised that it was a *'wind up'*.

After that he was nicknamed, *'Yorick.'*"

'There's no need to shout'

"On one occasion a man entered the front office of a police station and asked to see an officer from the Firearms Department. The wily office man went off and found the officer, but told him that his visitor was deaf and that he would need to shout to be heard. He then went back to the visitor and told him that because the firearms officer had been routinely exposed to weapons being fired, he was deaf and that the visitor would need to shout.

He then sat back and enjoyed the spectacle of two grown men shouting at each other!"

'Wrong time-right place'

"In about 1990, I was the office-man at Walsall, on one bitterly cold winter's night, at about 2am, when a tramp came into the station and asked if he could come in to stay out of the cold.

There used to be a small sectioned-off glass-fronted area as a waiting place for the Coroner's Officers and as I had control of the door-lock I allowed him in to go into that area.

He seemed grateful and lay down on the bench in there and dozed off.

A few hours later one of the Coroner's Officers happened to come in, and to my horror found that the old chap had passed away.

You can imagine the hassle that caused, having someone die on police premises, and in due course I was summoned to see the Chief Inspector for some advice.

I did it out of compassion really but was subjected to some *'ribbing'* for a few weeks after.

That said if he was going to go, there was probably no better place to be dealt with than right outside that door!"

'Getting an ear full'

"A very silly, (but endlessly amusing), *'blag'*, was one of putting black fingerprint ink on the inside of a telephone earpiece. The perpetrator would then dial the number from across the office and watch as someone randomly picked it up.

That person would then usually walk around completely unaware that their ear was covered in ink!"

'Proper 'characters''

"Two characters spring to mind that were both *'legends'* in their time: This is a long time ago when Policing was very different.

The first officer was once heard to say, *'Don't worry Luv, it's only me little stick of Blackpool Rock'*, after a lady bus passenger jumped as she sat next to him and onto his *'peg'* (wooden truncheon) in his inside trouser pocket.

This officer was very well known on the old *'F'* Division, (Birmingham City Centre), for riding his bike in full uniform into pubs, having a drink, and then riding out again.

He was once sent out with a message by the CID to get a parent in for a juvenile prisoner, only to be found at the house an hour later, playing football with his helmet with the other kids!

He was once convicted of failing to stop at the scene of an accident when he crashed his car into a milk float, and whilst on the Accident Enquiry Squad, he personally went to another Force area to make enquiries instead of sending a letter.

When he was the office-man at Edward Rd, he would get a *'Pro Con'* to man the office whilst he went for a *'pee'*, only to disappear to the local *'boozer'*.

A local resident once complained to the Superintendent at Kings Heath about the *'resident owl'* at Edward Road *'nick'* keeping her awake at night with its constant *'hooting'*.

It turned out that this *'hooting'* only occurred when the said officer was the office-man on nights!

He eventually was moved to Lloyd House HQ on security, where he was known to offer all and sundry a mint.

The second officer could be equally unorthodox, *'Madam, put your wagons in a circle and I'll send the cavalry,'* was the answer a woman got from a Sergeant at Belgrave Rd, when she telephoned to complain that the Indians were fighting in the street again.

He was very talented and could recite Shakespeare. He was also often heard singing opera in the street at night.

His most talked about escapade was when he was on nights in the office at Belgrave Road Police Station. He was having a rummage through the Detained Property Store and came across a couple of candlesticks and a ceremonial sword.

He grabbed the station *'Union Jack'* flag, and laid himself out *'in state'* on the front- office counter. Allegedly a man came into the *'nick'* and saw this tableau in front of him, whereupon with his eyes rolling he leapt into the air and out of the front door, when the officer winked at him!

I only met him once, when I saw this scruffy unshaven apparition sitting in the controller's space at Belgrave, with an equally scruffy dog sitting beside him.

I questioned if the kennels were in quarantine, and whether strays had to be kept in the station, only to be told that it was his dog!"

'Meet The Beetles'

"When I was a young *'bobby'*, a colleague showed me how to make a little device that could cause much mirth.

Back in those days there were three posters in the reception of every *'nick'*, namely a bicycle identification poster, a dog identification poster and a Colorado Beetle poster.

The Colorado Beetle can devastate potato crops and back in the 70/80s the Government were very concerned about them. All young *'bobbies'* would have seen these posters.

Anyway, back to the device – we'd snip the top off a wire coat-hanger so that you had a U-shaped piece of wire. Then you would get a small elastic band and a button roughly the size of a two pence piece. The elastic band was threaded through the button which was then superglued to the ends of the U-shaped wire.

Then we would write *'Dead Colorado Beetle'* on a small envelope and wind up the button about a hundred times before placing it carefully inside.

The *'device'* was then slid into the envelope and couldn't unwind as it was contained with a small flat surface.

Officers would stroll into the front office, spot the envelope, and enquire as to its origins, only to be told that it had been brought in by an old lady and definitely confirmed as being a Colorado Beetle.

Not many officers could control their curiosity, and would often ask to have a look at it – to which of course I was only too happy to comply.

As they would pucker the envelope open, the button would be released, causing high repetition clicking.

There would be much screaming and crying as the envelope often found itself on the floor followed by hysterical laughing once they realised that they hadn't actually been attacked by a beetle which had come back to life."

'Stationary traffic'

'One day we were working together in the taxi rank on the forecourt of the station. (British Transport Police).

Most of the commuters would rush up and take a taxi. The taxis would not queue so we usually ended up with taxis spilling into Stephenson Street, thus blocking that street and causing complaints from our colleagues in the City of Birmingham Police.

Hence, we had to ensure that the taxis took their proper place at the head of the queue. My elderly colleague on this day shouted to the taxi drivers, *'Pull em down'*.

A woman looked at him a bit funny and quick as a flash he said to her, *'No. Not you dear'*.

Another *'party trick'* of his, was to stop the ascending escalators from the station concourse to the Birmingham Shopping Centre during the morning rush-hour when they were full of commuters. The passengers would leave a train, come up from the platforms en-block, and go through the ticket barrier before stepping onto the escalators, whilst reading their newspapers. My colleague would then stop the escalators and it would take a few seconds for the commuters to realise that the escalators had stopped. They were not amused."

'Quick thinking'

"In 1973, along with other officers, I went to a fellow officer's stag night.

We finished duty at 14.30 hours and went to the Railway Club at Monument Lane. At 23.00 hours, we then went to *'The Peter Rabbit'* Club in Broad Street. We left there at about 04.00 hours the following morning.

A Detective Constable dropped me off at my Mother-in-Law's where the wife and I were staying. I tried to creep in, but the wife heard me open the door and asked what I was doing. I told her that I was just going out on *'Rest Day'* working. I went back to the city-centre, had some breakfast, and returned home stating that my duty had been cancelled!"

'A Yen for it'

(British Transport Police). "In 1974 there was a Detective Constable at Coventry where I was working. He was one of the *'old school'*. He was still paid weekly and drew his wages on a Thursday from the Booking Office.

Another officer at Coventry with me was a great joker. We were on the same wavelength and shared the same sense of humour. The police service at that time was well known for playing jokes on colleagues.

The CID officer was very anti-Japanese. He served in the Second World War but never spoke about his service and I suspect that he might have been a Prisoner of War. At this time, I had some old Japanese Yen which I kept at home. My colleague and I hatched a plot to play a joke on our colleague and I brought the Yen into the office and kept it in my locker until I saw my chance.

One Thursday morning, the CID officer was typing up a prosecution file and when I said I was going out he asked me if I could get his wages. I took his card and drew his wages. I then obtained a blank wage slip and an empty wages envelope, and went to the Clerk's office, where I typed up the wage slip and wrapped it round the Japanese Yen and placed it in the envelope.

I returned to the office and the CID officer stopped what he was doing. He always insisted on counting his money. It didn't matter if he was interviewing a triple murderer, he would stop.

He opened the envelope and, on seeing the Yen, he came out with a number of expletives and was coughing and sputtering. When he had calmed down we got a *'bollocking'* from the Detective Sergeant.

Another trick we played on him was cutting two eye-holes in a newspaper. The CID officer was a reader of the *'Daily Express'*, which in those days was a broadsheet. He would usually dispose of it in the litter bin before he went home.

We retrieved one and kept it back, so as not to damage his current one. My colleague and I cut two eye holes in this paper and awaited our chance. It came along one morning when the CID officer announced that he was going to go on the station concourse to carry out some observations.

We knew that he would take his newspaper with him and we swopped the papers over without him knowing. When he came back there were a few expletives. He took it all in good part and saw the funny side."

'Blue is the colour'

"We used Securicor for all of our vehicle servicing, and at the British Transport Police office at Wolverhampton we drove a dark blue MK 1 Escort. One night in the 1970s, about two weeks before Christmas, one of the West Midlands Police area car drivers came into my office in a state.

I was treated like one of the shift at most of the local *'nicks'* and got on well with them.

The officer had reversed and scraped along a concrete post and made a right mess of one side of the Allegro.

I mentioned that Securicor had a spray booth and may help. Off we went to the depot and the manager was spoken to nicely.

He arranged for the lads to clean up the damage and spray the panels but said that he would need a couple of hours to do even a *'rush job'*.

To cover for the officer, we jumped into my BTP vehicle and then responded to all of his calls until the end of his shift.

We got back to Securicor at about 5.30am and the *'spray man'* said that he had been having some difficulties in getting an exact colour match but that he thought it was close enough.

The car was duly parked at the far end of the local police yard and we booked off at 6am with a sigh of relief, whilst it was still dark.

Next night the officer came back to give me an update. Apparently, it appeared that under artificial lights the colours were well off and the respray was very obvious. Luckily it was that bad that the early-turn officers had taken the view that it must have been the subject of graffiti and told officers to watch out for repeat attacks!

Years later I bumped into the officer at a social function and found that he had retired. Ironically he was working in transport management."

'A gift-horse in the mouth'

"One evening, one of the uniformed officers was checking the waiting rooms on Leicester Railway Station and he came across a woman who was breast-feeding her baby.

The baby was reluctant to take the mother's milk and she said to the baby, *'If you don't want it this nice policeman will have it.'*

The look on the officer's face was an absolute picture –

I wish I had my camera with me."

'Good Intentions'

"I was late-duty Inspector at Birmingham New Street Station sometime in the late 1970's, and after getting *'suited and booted'*, strolled into the Information Room (I.R.) where a Constable colleague was sat behind a console.

He was watching something intently on the CCTV screen and when I asked him about it, he said that the West Midlands Police had carried out an anti-terrorism exercise on the front-yard of the station that morning, and that he was watching the CCTV footage of the incident.

We were both aware of someone coming into the I.R. but didn't pay any attention as we were engrossed in what was on the screen. Suddenly the door of the I.R. slammed shut and I looked up to see a figure dash through the open doorway leading to the stairs exiting the police office complex.

I could hear hurried footsteps on the stairs. A few moments later another officer came up the stairs and through the door asking why one of the Sergeants was running. I told him that I had no idea and went back to watching the TV screen.

Probably ten or fifteen minutes later a very red-faced and sweating Sergeant came back up the stairs and almost staggered into the vestibule in front of the I.R. counter.

He just about managed to gasp out, *'Where's the incident then?'* Or words to that effect.

I asked him what he'd been doing and he said that he'd seen the police action on the TV screen and had raced downstairs to see if he could assist. After a fruitless search of the front yard, he'd returned to the office. I couldn't help laughing but thanked him for his concern and pointed out that what he had seen wasn't live, but a recording of an exercise.

Apart from the three of us I can't remember if anyone else in the office was aware of this at the time but I'm sure that the *'office telegraph'* soon had a version of events doing the rounds, although he couldn't be faulted for his sense of duty and eagerness to get stuck-in!"

'Deputy Dawg'

"In 1976, whilst I was serving at Leicester, I had an Old English sheepdog as a pet and on occasions I would take him on the train when visiting the family in Lancashire.

One day I had a laugh with one of the railway staff who, shall I say, was a little gullible.

He saw me, on the train with my dog and said to me that it was unusual to see me on the train with a dog.

I told him that as I was a C.I.D officer, this was a German Shepherd in disguise and we were on a case.

He seemed to believe me and often asked if I still used the dog for duty."

'The phantom key-jangler'

"At Bilston Street, (Wolverhampton), custody block you had to go down a flight of steps to the bottom, and then go through a set of security doors which had a code.

A few feet away there were the gaoler type barred gates which the custody officer, or assistant, had to come and unlock with keys to allow entry.

Sometimes officers going to the block would forget the code so the custody officer would have to walk twenty to thirty feet from the comfort of the rest area to unlock the gates and open the security doors.

When it was quiet some officers would rattle the door handles and then run off up the stairs and out of sight, much to the annoyance of one particular custody officer who, having opened the doors and found no-one there would chunter on about being disturbed and was not happy.

If you were subtle about it you could do it a few times without him realising – or least ways he never let on."

'The burning question'

"In 1967, on traffic, I was with my shift partner, a PC who eventually became HMI. (Her Majesty's Inspector). He was a smashing bloke, a great officer. and a pleasure to work with.

One break time, we were in the refreshments room with an older, (in years and service), borough officer who was quietly reading his newspaper. My partner lit the grill, and placed his bread in there to toast.

Just then, the office man rang and wanted us to answer some query relative to an HORT/2, (better known as a 'producer' for driving documents).

On leaving the refs room my partner said to the borough officer, *'Could you watch my toast please?'* *'Sure'*, he replied. After a few minutes, we returned to the room.

Upon opening the door, we were met by clouds of black smoke and the smell of burning. The toast was still under the grill, and on fire.

My mate rushed across, turned out the gas, blew out the flames then said to the borough officer who was still nonchalantly reading his paper, *'I thought you said you would watch my toast?'*

The reply came, *'I did. It started to smell, went black, and then set fire to itself, that's about the full story. OK? Do you want my paper?'* He then left the room.

Brilliant, he never cracked a smile."

'No more left in the box'

"I used to work for a time as a PNC (Police National Computer) operator at F1 Sub-Division control in the late 1970s, before the Edmund Davis report (which upped pay and improved working conditions for officers), when the number of officers in the job was probably at its lowest. Birmingham City Centre, especially on a 2-10pm shift, used to get very busy, and logs came at us from the Force Central Control Room, *'Yankee Mike,'* in 'droves', with no-one to send.

'Yankee Mike' were constantly asking us when we could deal with the logs.

One Sergeant Controller used to take this for a while then send a log across to the Control Room stating,

'In about half an hour gents. Have just put another box of dehydrated constables into soak and they will take that long to activate.'

It always stopped the flow for a little while until they could come up with a reply which seldom happened."

'The mystery cabinet'

"In the 1970's Her Majesty's Inspector, (HMI), when inspecting the West Midlands force, wished to know what back-up system we had for our computerised Command and Control system. We never saw the HMI but his thoughts circulated around the control room community.

Weeks afterwards, a metal office cabinet arrived at the FI, (Steelhouse Lane), control room. It was locked and had a force badge on the door with a printed note stating, *'Angus Mk 2 command and control system only to be used in an emergency - key in station-safe.'*

Well no-one seemed to know anything about this, so the cabinet was finally opened to reveal that it was multi-shelved with just one pencil and a notepad on one shelf, with *'Angus Mk 2 log book'* written on it.

We all had a chuckle, including the Superintendent when he got to hear of it – before he had it removed!"

'The 'Lazarus' duck'

"One morning, I was driving along a very quiet country lane, it was in the middle of the summer and I was full of the joys of life.

Suddenly a large duck flew out of the hedge directly into the path of my car and I hit it full on.

I stopped and went to see if it was alive and found it lying in the middle of the road – stone-dead.

I knew that one of the blokes was into 'road kill' so I picked this duck up and placed it into the front foot-well of the car and carried on with my patrol.

Sometime later I was returning to the *'nick'* for refreshments and had just turned into the station yard. Suddenly this 'dead duck' came back from beyond. The first thing I knew was that there was something flying around the interior of the car at about 100mph.

I was startled and not knowing what was going on I bailed out of the car, which was still moving forward until it came to rest against the station wall. The duck by this time had spotted its chance and was last seen flying out into the street."

'Unnatural sex'

"Out in the County you got some very different crimes to in the City. One of my colleagues arrested an individual for bestiality with a horse.

After the defendant was interviewed, I was talking to my colleague and asked him about the interview, which he informed me went along the following lines:

Officer, 'Why did you do it?'

Reply, 'Because I thought that the horse would enjoy it.'

Officer, 'How did you manage to penetrate the horse?'

Reply, 'By standing on a bale of straw.'

Officer, 'Was the horse male or female?'

Reply, 'Female of course... what do you think I am? Kinky!!'

'Boris the Badger'

"Shortly after 11pm one evening, two armed response officers, together with a male and female colleague, in another vehicle, were sent to Greenhill in Evesham following a report of two men climbing a fence and trying to break into a house.

On arrival at the scene they found two men covered in blood sat on top of a fence, who refused to come down when requested. They claimed that they had been riding their bikes along the road when they were attacked and bitten by a large badger.

One of the Firearms officers, being an untrusting sort of chap, went into the garden of the house to check the property and seconds later was seen vaulting over a six-foot-high fence shouting *'It's coming, it's coming!'*

Two seconds later, a badger ran out of the gateway and chased the officer around his patrol car. Both Firearms officers rapidly climbed onto the bonnet of their car in an effort to escape as the badger tried to get onto the bonnet to bite them.

The officers then mounted the roof of the car, whilst a nearby householder phoned the police to say that a *'badger was attacking the officers.'*

The officers couldn't even 'self-arm' to protect themselves and the public, as they couldn't get to the ground to open the car doors.

As the other two officers arrived, and got out of their vehicle, the badger started chasing the female officer around the car. It managed to bite her trousers and she duly climbed onto the roof of the second police car as it continued to try and reach her.

Whilst this was going on, her police partner crept up behind the badger and hit it on the head with his *'PR24'* baton.

The badger sank to its knees and for sixty seconds appeared to have been knocked out - until it woke up and recommenced its attack.

In the meantime, an ambulance arrived, and the crew observed the police officers, plus by now the two men from the fence, all standing on the roofs of the police vehicles. They retreated, laughing all the way.

The badger then wandered off out of sight.

The next night it returned, and this time attacked a female walking her dog, who was admitted to hospital with serious leg injuries. He then attacked a man who opened his front door to see what was going on, and he was so seriously bitten around the arms and legs that he had to be admitted to Selly Oak Hospital for skin graft surgery.

The badger, which turned out to have been 'hand-reared', was later captured by an expert and taken away. The story made the national news and one of the officers was later quoted. *'I looked at him, he looked at me, and then he came running at me with all those teeth. I didn't realise that they could run so fast.'"*

'Taking the piss'

"After completing my twenty weeks training at Hendon, having joined the Metropolitan Police, I was posted to 'street duties' for ten weeks at a busy London station.

One day I was given a copy of a *'telex'* message which bore a list of *'WPC* names I had been with on my initial training course. The gist of the telex message was that a male officer had made a complaint that whilst on the same course he had slept with a female officer, following which he had contracted a sexually transmitted disease, otherwise known as an *'STD'*.

In order to progress the *'complaint'* every female officer was requested to provide a *'water sample'* and to take it to the Complaints & Discipline Department which had offices at Tintagel House by the Embankment. I was furious about the request, and so mad because I knew it couldn't be me, but being young in service I just accepted it as being genuine.

On a couple of occasions, I tried to get a sample, but found that I was so worked up about it that I just couldn't do it.

Finally, I managed, and off I went to Tintagel House with my little container.

On arrival in the reception I explained the purpose of my visit and was handed a note which was from my Sergeant. When I looked at the note it read simply, *'Now that's what I call really call taking the piss!'*"

'Facing the truth'

"I remember being posted as a gaoler at a South East London Police Station back in the early 90's.

A Detective had been posted from one of the squads, on a temporary basis, and was dealing with a suspect for a residential burglary.

He had charged the man and was in the process of doing fingerprints and photographs when he called out for some more ink.

As the Detective finished taking the fingerprints, he turned to me and said, *'Right, could you ink up his face now?'*

Me and the suspect turned to each other and looked equally confused.

The Detective said, *'We think the suspect put his face up against the glass window at the back before he broke in – so we want to match up the face prints.'*

He then started smearing ink over the suspects face and asked me to spread it about a bit using the ink roller adding, *'Make sure that you get around his ears too.'*

Once the officer was satisfied that his suspect was suitably *'inked up'* he proceeded to roll the man's face over a sheet of A4 paper, whilst holding the back of his head. The result was actually quite impressive.

The officer concluded, *'Right you can clean it up now,'* and handed the suspect a piece of toilet paper before asking me to return him to a cell.

As I returned from the cell area the Detective, who had remained straight-faced throughout the episode, looked at me and simply winked.

Shortly afterwards he returned to his previous posting."

'A forensic search'

"Whilst on a response shift, an offence of Robbery was reported during the day, and one of the brand-new probationers was tasked with doing a search of the area to try to find a can of *'Coke'* which the victim remembered the 'offender' holding at the time.

What the probationer did not know was that prior to being tasked other members of the shift had gone down to Brixton Road and strategically placed loads of empty cans of *'Coke'* in the area.

He duly returned carrying three or four huge *'evidence bags'* containing cans of *'Coke.'*"

'That sinking feeling'

"On Sandwell Valley there is a beautiful balancing lake which in an urban setting is a lovely peaceful place to watch the sunrise, and for officers to contemplate the previous busy night of police action.

The lake is equipped with a boat slipway which is a gentle slope made of concrete used to launch boats.

Two officers decided one night to park their police patrol car on the slipway and there was a sneaking suspicion that they may have fallen asleep for a few moments.

Describing it later to his Sergeant one of the officers said, *'the car suddenly went very dark and the previously translucent windows went a very dark grey in colour.'*

The awful reality of what had happened to them was brought brutally home as water cascaded into the car until it was totally flooded, allowing the officers to escape, although completely soaked.

The officers summoned their Sergeant to the scene and he arrived just in time to glimpse the police blue light of the vehicle just visible offshore.

Despite their best efforts to conjure up an explanation that the vehicle's handbrake had become somehow released, both were duly brought before the local Superintendent to determine what their punishment should be.

Being somewhat experienced in the ways of life he said, *'If we could swap places, how would you deal with this?'*

The less stupid of the officers *'chanced his arm'* and said, *'I'd give us a really good telling off and 'ground us' from driving for a month.'*

The Superintendent said, *'Done – now get out!'"*

'Chasing the bandit'

"I was on nights posted to *'FZ1'*, (fast response car, city centre), together with another officer. I was the only 'Advanced Driver' on the shift and he could only drive the *'Zulu'* as long as I was with him, as he was only a 'Standard' graded driver. The *'Zulus'* were fitted with both Divisional and Force radio communication systems

It would have been about 1985, and about 1am in the morning, when we came across a mustard coloured Ford Capri 2.8i, parked up in Holiday Street. Those 2.8i Capri's were very desirable for car thieves as they were very quick, and easy to steal.

When we checked the car, it had been *'barrelled'*, and a subsequent check on *'PNC'* revealed that it was a stolen vehicle.

There was no one with it, so we decided to recover it to the stolen vehicle pound at Bridge Street West Police station.

As Bridge Street West Police station was only open from 7am to 10pm, it was decided that the other officer would drive the Capri, whilst I would have to go to Steelhouse Lane to collect the pound keys to open it up.

All of our radio transmissions regarding the Capri had been passed via the Divisional radio, who would update the *'PNC'* with a *'found report'* once we got to the pound.

The other officer, being a reckless sort, realised that it would take me a few minutes to collect the keys and to open the Pound, so he decided to give this Capri a spin around the city.

Unknown to both of us, the shift Inspector, who was an Advanced driver, had taken out the spare *'Zulu'* as the supervision car, and it wasn't long before his attention was drawn towards a mustard coloured 2.8i Ford Capri, being driven very fast around the city.

Being single-manned, it was easier for him to use the Force radio in the *'Zulu'* and requested a *'PNC'* check on the Capri, which came back as a stolen vehicle as Division had not yet updated *'PNC'* with the *'found report'*.

Needless to say, our Inspector now had a stolen vehicle that was refusing to stop.

By this time, I had opened up the gates to the Pound and was awaiting the arrival of the other officer but as I was out of my car, I was unaware of this chase being broadcast on the car's Force radio, which the local traffic police cars were now making towards.

I then got back in the car and could hear this commentary of the stolen vehicle, failing to stop, which ironically was heading towards my location.

I had missed the start so I had no idea what vehicle it was, just the locations and the excessive speeds. *'Hurry up, we may get in on the end of this one!'* I was thinking.

After a few seconds, I saw the Capri that we had recovered from Holiday Street, come *'piss-balling'* towards me, being driven by the other officer, followed by a stream of *'blue lights'*, as it pulled into the Pound, virtually on two wheels.

The officer saw me sitting outside, his eyes went wide-open and the blood drained from his face as he skidded to a halt inside the Pound.

It transpired that he had thought that it was me who had been chasing him and for a bit of sport, had decided to *'tank it'* around the city.

To say that the Inspector was unimpressed was a huge understatement.

I had one of the biggest *'bollockings'* of my service, just for collecting the keys and opening the Pound, and he threatened the other officer with all sorts of disciplinary and Road Traffic Act offences.

The other guy never worked on the *'Zulu'* with me again!"

'The last 'Bungy' jump'

"A youth went into Netherton Woods intent on killing himself by hanging.

Unfortunately, there was a fundamental flaw in his planning as he used a *'bungy'* rope so that when he jumped out of a tree, he hit the ground and was immediately catapulted back up, banging his head on a stout branch.

The lump on his head took his mind off his previous woes and he lived to fight another day. *"*

'A play on words'

"A colleague and I attended the address of one of our regular *'customers'* in the Black Country, in order to execute a warrant.

On the way to the house we discussed how his mother could be less than pleasant towards the police and always covered for her son.

We knocked the door and it burst open. There was said mother standing there in her usual dishevelled state, hair all over the place, and cigarette in hand.

The first words out of her mouth in her broad Midlands accent were, *'What the fuck do yow pair want?'*

I asked if her son was in, but due to our earlier conversation my colleague started to smile.

She looked at him and said, *'What the fuck are you smiling at?'*

He insisted he wasn't but she said to me, *'He's smirkin at me.'*

I said, *'No he's not, you're smirking.'*

She squared up to me and said, *'No I'm not.'*

I kept a straight face and said, *'Yes you are. You're smirking a fag.'*

At this point my partner collapsed in a fit of laughter whereupon his mother told us to *'fuck off'* and slammed the door shut.

The joys of accents."

'It's no yolk'

"In 1998 I was the Sector Inspector at Fletchamstead Highway Police Station, (Coventry). We had raided the home of a rare bird's egg thief the day before, got lots of eggs back and arrested the *'tea leaf'*.

I was told by the Royal Society of the Protection of Birds, (RSPB), that there would be loads of press interest. This was true and I did TV and radio interviews but the one that *'killed me'* was the first.

I arrived early next morning at 0645hrs, and spoke to a DJ from local BBC, *'Radio One'* I think, gave him all the *'guff'* and then came the question *'What should the public do if they suspect that someone is an egg thief?'*

I rattled off the usual about contacting the local police, or said that they could of course contact the Crime Stoppers 'hot-line'.

The DJ responded, *'Thanks for all that Inspector. Just remind us what the Crime Stoppers number is please?'*

Bugger it, I thought, as I scuttled around the office trying to find any paperwork with it on, and pulled the phone off the desk as I strained to look through the window at the police vehicles in the yard below, as all of them had the number on them.

I couldn't see one. I finished up with some lame request that people could find the number in the phonebook and thought, *'not my finest hour'*, but hopefully no-one at the station will have heard it.

How wrong I was, as a couple of hours later I walked into the CID office at Chase Avenue in Coventry to much hilarity. A Detective Sergeant who was an early riser had heard the whole of the interview on the radio on his way into work.

I was later presented with a plastic egg for my troubles which I have to this day."

'The truth and nothing but the truth'

"This story was knocking about on the old *'A'* and *'F'* divisions in Birmingham City Centre for years. Apparently there used to be a magistrate at Birmingham who did not like officers to repeat offender's swear words in court and used to ask for the comments to be written down and handed to the bench.

On one such occasion a dog handler did this, handing the paper containing the offending comment to the bench. At this point the officer was asked what happened next, to which the officer replied, *'Then he kicked my fucking dog your worship.'"*

'Official' No *Blag'*

"The following is a true story that happened to me.

Circa 1973 I was the 'night DC' for the *'B'* Division and my Sergeant was the 'night DS' covering *'B'* and *'A'* Divisions. (Birmingham inner city and central).

We booked on and joined the day staff in the pub to catch up with what had been going on. We then returned to Belgrave Road, to be told we were required at Woodbridge Road, (both Police stations), where a headless body had been found in a driveway off Anderson Park Road.

We thought it was a *'wind up'* at first, but on attending we learned that a couple had returned home to find the naked headless torso of a young woman in their driveway. They had thought it was a mannequin at first.

One thing led to another, and a suspect was arrested nearby, who eventually confessed to the decapitation. However, he couldn't be specific as to where the head was. He said he had put it in a bag, and put the bag in a dustbin at one of the houses in the surrounding area. By this time, it was gone 4.00 am.

The Head of CID was in charge, so he split the detectives into teams of two to search all the surrounding house's dustbins. My Sergeant, who is sadly no longer with us, was known as the *'male model'*, as he was always immaculate; he was not too keen on rummaging through dustbins at 4.00 am in the dark!

Off we went, alternating houses to be quicker. After about an hour, with continual grumbling from my colleague, he suddenly stopped at the gate of one of the houses in Woodstock Rd, and said that he couldn't *'do this one'*.

I told him to stop pissing about, because if we didn't find the head, we would have another dead body on our hands when some old lady found it and had a heart attack! However, he was insistent that he couldn't do it.

I pushed past him and lifted the lid, at which point he screamed!

I said, *'You are really pissing me off now.'*

He said, *'No, it's there!'* And it was!

It had been mutilated, so no wonder he screamed.

How he knew, at the bottom of the path, that it was the right house, he was never able to explain.

On the way home, later that morning, I was listening to *'Children's Choice'* on the radio, and the presenter said he had a request from someone at Headless Cross, near Redditch. I was at the traffic lights at Tally Ho! Police Training Centre and just burst into laughter! Other motorists must have thought I was *'crackers.'"*

'The born interviewer'

"I had a *'Pro Con'* who I had to assess. I looked through his workload and he had an outstanding enquiry of a nasty dog bite on a small child. I asked him to arrange appointments with the victim's mother and the owner of the offending dog.

On a Sunday morning we went to the home of the victim where a very small young lady answered the door.

The *'Pro Con'* was obviously very nervous with me allowing him to take the lead. He said to this young lady, who obviously had dwarfism, *'Is your Mommy in?'*

She replied that her mother didn't live there but asked if we wanted to see her daughter's injuries as a result of the dog bite.

It was then that he *'twigged'* that this was in fact the mother. I didn't say anything but I had a little chuckle to myself.

We did the business there and then went to the owner of the dog's house. Here was a young woman and her dog which was obviously a child substitute as it walked around with a *'dolly'* in its mouth.

Again, all of the official business was done and we were just about to leave when the *'Pro Con'* looked at me as if to ask had he missed anything. I just looked at him and said to the woman, *'How old is the dog?'* She replied with an age to which the young officer said, *'Is that in human years or 'doggie' years?'*

I was in stitches but tried to hide it.

Now this was in the days when there were Bars in police stations. We were due to finish at 2pm and we all normally had a drink before going home.

Just before we got back to the station the officer said to me, *'You won't say anything about what just happened to the rest of the shift will you?'* I said, *'Of course not.'*

Guess what the first subject of conversation was in the bar?"

'Wheel's on fire'

"I was on a Traffic patrol double crewed, on an evening shift during school holidays in Worksop, North Notts. Radio communications at that time were not the best, and the Fire Service used the same Frequency and channels as the police.

It was a nice warm summer evening. You always expect a bit of bother with kids when on holiday, (in the 60s, it was mostly devilment).

Then a call came from a Leading Fire Officer who was a large man with a very broad Yorkshire/Derbyshire accent. 'Ello. Leading Fire Officer X, en route to a reported fire in the bandstand at Langold Lakes.'

This was a large park area with a bandstand in the centre of an island, surrounded by a moat about 15' wide.

Access was via a bridge made from railway sleepers, with no guard rails..

'10/4.' (received), came the reply from NH (Notts control) It was now raining. About 10 minutes later...

'Ello NH, Leading Fire Officer X here again. I make a request for a light recovery vehicle to attend this location.as we have tried to negotiate the bridge, it's pissing down with rain, and the tender's rear wheels are hanging over side of bridge.'

NH: '10/4 stand by.' 10 mins later........

'Ello NH, Leading Fire Officer X here again. Reference my last message, can you substitute light recovery for heavy recovery as we've fell into the bloody water.'"

'Doing drugs'

'When I was a Detective Sergeant at Steelhouse Lane, I arrested a bloke for illegal possession of a firearm and ammunition. Because he came from Hereford, I asked the local West Mercia CID to *'turn his drum'* over for me. (Search his house).

I was interviewing the prisoner when the Hereford DC rang back with his findings. He said that he had found numerous items concerning firearms, including telescopic sights, bullet making equipment, empty shell cases, jars of black powder, jars of brown powder and two jars of white powder that he had been unable to identify despite having sniffed and tasted the contents.

I asked the prisoner what they were, and after the DC had described the jars, he replied that the white powder was the remains of his parents!"

'Police tongue-twister'

"An old *'chestnut'*. What's the difference between a magician's wand and a policeman's truncheon? – answer – one is used for *'cunning stunts.'*

'By the balls'

"Another old story that constantly did the rounds. A police officer attended a house and was met by a furiously barking dog. A woman leant out of an upstairs window and told the officer that the dog was harmless but that he should just kick his balls.

The next thing was that the dog took off propelled by the officer's boot.

The woman cried out, *"I really wanted you to kick his rubber balls on the front lawn!"*" (I believe Jasper Carrot stole this one – or was it the other way around?).

'All bark and..'

"Rumour had it that a certain dog handler, renowned for liking a pint, had lost his German Shepherd police dog when it ran off after a road accident.

Despite a lengthy search he couldn't find it, so the following night he took his own Jack Russell terrier, which constantly barked, out in the back of the police van.

The dog man told his colleagues that the dog had a sore throat and couldn't work, and so refused to take it out of the van.

Four days later the German Shepherd returned."

'Licked into shape'

"The Force helicopter was forced to land in a field between Frankley Reservoir and the M5 one day, due to technical difficulties.

The company responsible for its maintenance were from Gloucester and we were tasked to look after it overnight until they could get there.

A double-crewed car was deployed on nights to keep an eye on it. It would appear that the *'God of Sleep'* got the best of the officers, who woke up in daylight to find that they were surrounded by a herd of cows.

During the night the cows had licked off all of the livery and insignia from the helicopter as it must have contained salt or something similar. The officers had some difficult questions to answer!"

'Having kittens'

"One afternoon on a late turn, I conducted the parade and two of the officers immediately disappeared and returned a couple of hours later grinning like *'Cheshire cats.'*

I asked them where they had been and they told me that they had been to see the *'Atomic Kittens'* a very popular and beautiful female band.

Apparently, some youngster on the Beechdale Estate had won a competition and the prize was for the group to sing one of their songs in his house.

The two officers provided the *'community policing'* aspect to the visit!

I told them off – for not involving me!"

'A question of boundaries'

"Rumours have abounded over the years as to boundary 'issues' when dealing with incidents. Wolverhampton High Level rail station is actually above the main Staffs and Worcester canal. In the 1970s it was the border between the West Midlands Police areas of Wolverhampton and Willenhall.

One Sunday morning, a member of staff came to the office to report a body in the *'cut'*. (Canal). I breathed a sigh of relief as I knew it was on the *'locals'* (rather than British Transport Police), and put a call into the West Midlands Police communications room before switching to their channel and going out to get a statement from the person who had found it.

At that stage my belief was that it was floating on the Willenhall side but eventually the 'current' carried it to the Wolverhampton side and they finished up dealing with it."

'Rendering First-Aid'

"The CID at Smethwick had been looking for a long time to arrest a particular person, and on this particular day they were successful.

A couple of them were talking about it outside the Detective Chief Inspector's office. He heard them discussing the arrest and left his desk and stood in the doorway to clarify what he had heard.

After confirming the arrest, he got so excited that he jumped up in the air and hit the top of his head on the door frame, knocking himself out and cutting his head.

The office first-aider was called, who was a female, and at that time the only thing that she could find to place on top of the cut was a tampon which she put in place and tied around his chin.

He was duly taken off to hospital not knowing that he had a tampon firmly tied to the top of his head!"

'Handsworth is a dangerous place'

"Handsworth had a certain reputation in the 80's and 90's. The place ran on a knife-edge, and the slightest issue could spark a conflagration, as had happened with the riots. There was lots of trouble, drug dealing, murders, and firearms and other weapons were often brandished.

I was sent, as a young Inspector, to take charge of a response shift. As it happened, my first shift was the start of a set of nights.

It is quite a daunting thing to arrive at a new police station, meet a new shift, who are all assessing what level of 'wanker' you are (or not, hopefully) and get your head around the policing issues. Plus, you have to 'hit the ground running', and this was Handsworth – at night. Anything could happen to test me.

Things went ok to start with. I took Parade, met the shift and off they went on patrol. They were pretty experienced, many had worked Handsworth for years, and I had confidence in their abilities. I just hoped that I could earn their confidence and respect in turn.

After sorting a few things out in my office, I decided that the best thing to do would be to go out on patrol and to a few jobs to get the feel of the 'patch', and be with the boys and girls doing their stuff.

I reached into the top of my metal locker to get my flat cap, and struck my knuckle on an edge. It was sharp. When I examined the wound, I was taken aback to find that I had a deep cut, already bleeding profusely. I could see my knuckle bone. I knew what this meant, but I was in denial for a few minutes, before biting the bullet.

The Sergeant who took me to the General Hospital to be stitched lost no time in telling the whole shift that 'the gaffer' was being taken to hospital, and why.

That was the worst injury I ever received in Handsworth and I still have the scar to remind me of my first night in Handsworth. On a positive note, it did help 'break the ice' with the shift."

'Spilling the beans'

"My late husband worked on the motorway for a few years. One Saturday he was posted to Hilton Park services to make sure the travelling football fans didn't cause trouble. Whilst there he witnessed a young football fan ask for a *'fucking cup of coffee'*. The lady serving him charged him double, and when he pointed out the advertised price of coffee, she replied,

'That's for ordinary coffee son, 'fucking' coffee is dearer.'

Apparently, the young man walked away quietly without another word."

'Old Bill'

'Back in the 1970's, during my Drug Squad days, when I had hair, a beard and denims, we were staking out a house in Wolverhampton when we observed activity that we just could not leave.

The time was right for a *'bust'* but we knew that without a bulldozer it was almost impossible to enter.

Being the youngest, and looking the part, I volunteered to go and see if the door was open - or at least to see if there was any other way in. The rest of the team would wait out of sight and await my signal.

I was lucky, I followed someone in, and got through the outermost doors, when someone totally *'stoned'* said *'Who the fuck are you?'* I said, *'Bill'* and he went *'Oh okay.'*

I went back and opened the door to signal the others, and then walked back and the same person said, *'Bill who?'*

I said, *'Old Bill you're nicked.'*

It turned out to be the start of an investigation into a big conspiracy to import heroin. My evidence was given in court a few months later, which raised a few *'titters'* from the *'briefs'* and the Judge."

'Office ornaments'

"Whilst I was working as an Operational Command Unit Commander in 1997, we went through a challenging period where lots of effort was put into improving performance.

I went out one day and left the door of my office open. When I got back, I found a brand-new horse-riding whip placed in the middle of my desk.

I assumed that someone had loaned it from somewhere and was intent on giving me a 'message' as to how hard the officers were being made to work.

I judged that it would not be too hard to find out who was playing a *'blag'* on me but decided that it would be better not to respond in any way. I proudly displayed it henceforth in a prominent place and prayed that the culprit had been required to pay for the said item – no-one ever came forward to try to claim it.

Police officers tend to accumulate mementoes in the form of such things as pictures and certificates or trophies which are usually proudly displayed in their offices.

Just prior to being posted to Willenhall I was on an enquiry which resulted in a visit to the headquarters of the Freemasons in London. The staff there were very helpful and at the conclusion of the visit I was provided with a number of books on the subject.

I have never been a Freemason, but being a bit mischievous I duly placed all of these books, along with other mementoes, in a prominent place in the office.

I always watched with interest the reactions of visitors as they came across the books, – often interesting, but were they or weren't they? I never asked."

'Spending a penny'

"A certain Superintendent had his own toilet attached to the rear of his office. Someone placed a notice on the Ladies toilet saying, *'out of order'* and directing staff to use the Superintendent's toilet instead.

The senior officer spent the day wondering why there was a stream of women coming in and out of his toilet."

'Scouse humour'

"A member of the Royal Family was visiting Bloxwich Police Station, and the theme of the visit was very much about local people and local policing.

As the member of the Royal Family entered the police canteen, one officer who had a broad *'scouse'* accent was having his meal break.

She asked the officer where he lived, and in a somewhat belligerent tone he replied, *'I live at home with my mam.'*

Moving the VIP on swiftly, the officer received a glare filled with vengeful intent from the senior officer accompanying her, a certain Chief Superintendent Layton."

'Do you know who I am?'

"The phrase *'Do you know who I am?'* was generally a precursor to someone trying to establish their own sense of importance with a colleague.

History has it that a gentleman in plain clothes once presented himself to the office-man at Brownhills Police Station. The conversation went something like this:

Office-man, *'Good morning. How can I help you?'*

Visitor, *'Do you know who I am?'*

Office man, *'No. I haven't got a clue.'*

Visitor, *'Well, I am the new Assistant Chief Constable with Staffordshire Police and I have come to inspect the station.'*

Office-man, *'Well I am PC.....from the West Midlands Police, and Brownhills Police Station is in the West Midlands.'*

The visit didn't last very long."

Another variation: "Old Lags' knew better than to answer the phone and give their name – despite official exhortations to do so. On more than one occasion, a very senior officer has been upset at some facet of a telephone conversation with a PC and has uttered the immortal words

'Do you know who I am?'

The response *was 'No, do you know who I am?'*

'No'

'Well fuck off then.' Phone put down."

'Silent running'

"Officers attended an alarm one night in the Jewellery Quarter, and the Inspector and Sergeant were also present.

Whilst surrounding the premises, another officer turned up in a panda car, driving at speed with 'blues and two's', (sirens and blue lights), on.

The Inspector told the officer off for turning up like a 'Boeing 707' and scaring any burglars off. The Sergeant advised the officer about making a 'silent approach' when attending alarms.

Later that week the alarm went off at the British Rail Club in Sheepcote Street and officers attended.

This time the same officer turned up, and thirty yards from the scene switched his car engine off to make a silent approach.

In doing so the steering lock came on and he crashed into a wall."

'Murder in Malta'

"Three of us on the CID at Bradford Street had arrested a man for 'Wounding With Intent', and wanted to keep him in custody for court. For some reason the Detective Chief Inspector decided he should be bailed so he was released for a future court date.

One of the officers was seething, and we decided to *'blag'* the DCI. I did a fake telex purporting to be from the police in Malta, via Interpol, saying that they had researched our prisoner as requested.

They confirmed that he was wanted for murder and was not to be released as they were planning to extradite him.

The telex stated that a *'Captain Valetta'* was being dispatched immediately to formally arrest our suspect to comply with their legal procedures and would be arriving at Birmingham Airport within eight hours of the telex message.

It had all the usual stuff in it about no interviews to be conducted, clothing to be seized etc. despite it being a historical offence.

We left it on the DCI's desk, with a copy left in the station briefing book, and we all left the station, with only one person remaining manning the office, who was in on the *'blag'*.

The DCI came back, saw the message, and *'had it'* a treat.

He was trying to get hold of us, even to the point of sending radio messages to all officers to locate us urgently.

He was on his way to *'The Lane'*, intending to tell the Chief Superintendent, when he was told the truth – fair play he took it in good spirit."

'Public Speaking'

"I used to work with an Inspector who positively hated any form of public-speaking and was normally terrible at it. To help him keep his hands still, and to remember the main points, he used to use *'crib cards'* which he held in the palm of his hand.

We got on really well as a team, but on one occasion just prior to a big conference at Tally Ho! Police Training Centre, just as he was about to speak, he found that his cards were no longer in the right order and some were missing. He sat staring at us in the audience looking for signs of guilt!

On another occasion my work partner purchased a *'fart machine'* which worked in the form of a key fob. At a conference at Birmingham University, attended by about fifty people, it was attached to the underside lining of the Inspector's chair.

Every time he went to sit down the *'fart machine'* was activated.

He called for an early coffee break."

'It's no yolk again'

"One of my Detective Chief Inspectors knew someone who had chickens, and he always had twenty-four eggs delivered in a tray to his office every week.

I used to boil two or three in the kettle on *'lates',* (2 – 10pm shift), every week and put them back.

What I didn't know was that two other officers thought it was funny, and unbeknown to me had started to do the same thing.

It turns out that one week the DCI had only about two or three fresh eggs left in the tray!"

That's it for the stories and *'blags'*. But if you have any good ones, please send them to us via **hibostinbooks@gmail.com** and we will start on Volume II…..

Mike & Steve

Acknowledgements/References

The following serving and retired police officers from the West Midlands Police, British Transport Police and other Forces are especially thanked for their interest, support and contributions. Names have been removed from the excerpts to protect the guilty.

Bob Abson – retired West Midlands Police officer
Gary Ashby – retired West Midlands Police officer
Bob Ballantyne – retired West Midlands Police officer
Jeffrey Barley – retired West Midlands Police officer
David Bates – retired West Midlands Police officer
Chris Butler – former West Midlands Police officer
Graeme Clark – retired West Midlands Police officer
Mike Cresswell – retired West Midlands Police officer
Bill Croft – retired West Midlands Police officer
Robert C Davison – retired British Transport Police officer
Paul Dobbinson – retired West Midlands Police officer
Patrick Edwards – retired West Midlands Police officer
Tony (Bunny) Everett – retired West Midlands Police officer
David (*Fingers*) Faulkner – retired West Midlands Police officer
Mick Ferris – retired West Midlands Police officer
Ailean Freeman nee Macmillan – former Metropolitan Police officer
Brad Gilbey – retired West Midlands Police officer

Malcolm Griffin – retired West Midlands Police officer

Malcolm (*Doc*) Halliday – retired West Midlands Police officer

Frederick Halsey – retired West Midlands Police officer

Marcia Hardman – West Mercia Police staff

Stuart Harris – retired West Midlands Police officer

Pete *(Poobah)* Hill – retired West Midlands Police officer

Adrian (*Ada*) Howles – retired Birmingham City/West Midlands Police officer

Martin Hudson – retired West Midlands Police officer

'Humpo' – West Midlands Police

Paul Ingram – retired West Midlands Police officer

Dave Jinks – retired West Midlands Police officer

Davindra *(Dav)* Jisra – retired West Midlands Police officer

Kevin Kelsey – retired West Midlands Police officer

Pete Keys – retired West Midlands Police officer

Stuart Knight – retired West Midlands Police officer

Rebecca (*Becky*) Lee (nee Williams) – retired West Midlands Police officer

Jon Lighton – retired West Midlands Police officer

Paul McElhinney – retired West Midlands Police officer

Deb Menzel – retired West Midlands Police officer & member of the WMP Museum Group

Rob Moon – retired West Midlands Police officer

Stephen Murtagh – retired British Transport Police officer

Dave Newman – former Birmingham City and West Midlands Police officer (RIP)

Paul (*Rico*) Richards – retired West Midlands Police officer

David Rischmiller – retired West Midlands Police officer
Bill Rogerson – retired British Transport Police officer
Al Short – former West Mercia Police officer (*RIP*)
Allan Smith – retired West Midlands Police officer
Dave A. Smith – retired West Midlands police officer
Jan Such – retired West Midlands Police officer
Colin Tansley – retired West Midlands Police officer
Phil Tomlinson – Metropolitan Police officer
Brian Wainwright – retired Nottinghamshire Police officer
Nigel Walker – retired Warwickshire Police officer
Pete Walmsley – retired West Midlands Police officer
Andy Watson – former West Midlands Police officer

***

Cover photograph courtesy of Deb Menzel – West Midlands Police Museum Group

***

Addendum – Police slang

You will have noticed the regular usage of Police slang in the stories you have just read. Police officers talk like this without even realising it. We have provided translations wherever we can. If you would like further laughs, and to explore this subject further, please see:

'One In For D & D'

A little book containing more than five hundred and forty slang words, abbreviations, and nicknames used by police officers in the West Midlands from the 1970's onwards.

A light-hearted look at another aspect of the sub-culture of policing, which complements *'It's A Blag'* perfectly, both for those who have previously served in 'the job', or those with an interest in policing and humour.

The following are just a few examples - and are in large part additional to those within the book:

'AES' – Accident Enquiry Squad.

'Bending someone's ear' – engaging them in animated conversation.

'Blisters' – sometimes referring to the CID – they only turn up after the hard work has been done.

'BOHICA' – whenever yet another Force reorganisation was announced – *'Bend Over Here It Comes Again'*.

'Ching' or *'Ker Ching'* – extra money earned as a result of working overtime – comes from the sound made by a cash register.

'Cop a plea' – getting a *'guilty plea'* at court from a defendant. One officer recalls a case where a defence barrister made a plea to the Judge for his client to be given a sentence in months, rather than years, due to his guilty plea. The judge complied by sending the defendant to prison for thirty-six months.

'DCI' – Detective Chief Inspector.

'Dingly Dell' – cell.

'Go nap' – arrest someone.

'Grounded' – not allowed to drive police vehicles.

'Guff' – information.

'Hope you are not in any Xmas Clubs' – You will be in prison for Christmas.

'Lap Top' – a small police constable, (PC).

'NOD' – No Offences Disclosed.

'NTOA' – No Trace On Arrival.

'Niggle' – a popular card game in police canteens.

'Old Chestnut' – a story which has been told over and over again.

'Old Sweat' – long serving officer.

'PADFA' – Police Arrived Did Fuck All.

'PBO' – Permanent Beat Officer.

'Peterman' – a person who specialised in *'blowing'* safes with explosives.

'Rattle off' – provide the relevant information.

'Ribbing' – teasing.

'Rolling Over' – a suspect admitting their guilt during interview – alternatively known as a *'cough'.*

'Sprog' – new Probationary Constable.

'Suited and booted' – looking smart.

'The Box' – giving evidence on oath in court from the witness box. A retired officer recalls that on one occasion a defence barrister asked a CID officer if he was aware what happened if he did not tell the truth under oath. The officer responded, *'Yes a fairy will die.'* Apparently even the Judge had a giggle. On another occasion an officer asked if he could refresh his memory from the record of evidence in his pocket-note-book during a Crown Court case. When asked when he had made his notes up, he responded, *'I didn't make them up. They are true.'*

'The Domino King' – a Judge who dealt with offenders by means of sentencing in three and five years. Apparently one defendant who called the Judge this to his face received four years imprisonment.

'The Olympic Flame' – an officer who never goes out (of the station).

'The troops' – a number of police officers.

'Turkey Trot' – extra van patrols in the Small Heath area of Birmingham to protect butcher's shops in the run up to a Christmas period.

'Turning Queens' or *'Greasy Side Up'* – giving evidence against a co-accused.
'White Report' – miscellaneous police report.
'Woodentop' – uniformed officer.

The link for *'One In For D&D* on Amazon UK is https://www.amazon.co.uk/dp/198325567X/ and it is available as a paperback or Kindle ebook.

A note from the authors

If you enjoyed this book please take a moment to leave a review on its Amazon page. It will be greatly appreciated by us. If you want to know more about our Brummie/Midlands books, fiction and non-fiction, please visit and *'like'* our Facebook page *'Bostin Books'*, or our website *'bostinbooks.co.uk'*. We hope you enjoy them and many thanks for your support.

Michael Layton & Stephen Burrows 2018

Printed in Great Britain
by Amazon

32770988R00080